Prepping 123 - David Tuchman

A Reasonable and Rational, Step by Step, How-To Guide to Emergency Preparedness

ISBN-10: 1479287059
ISBN-13: 978-1479287055

Contents

Foreword

If you've become interested in prepping, then I'm sure you've started researching the subject on the internet. There are literally thousands of blogs and YouTube videos to spend your time on (or waste your time on, as the case may be). If you start now, you'll die of old age before you get through them all, as there's no end of people who will blather on for 10 or 15 minutes to give you one sentence worth of useful advice, if that! If you're like me, you'll quickly realize that you're going to have to waste an awful lot of time on these blogs looking for specific answers, and of course YouTube is filled with people who just love to hear themselves talk, but have very little, if anything, useful to say. A small percentage of them actually appear intoxicated. I've wasted 10 minutes watching a woman tell me she found weevils in her pasta, and then there was that guy who told me, in just 15 minutes, that the best gun to have is the one I like the feel of and can use well! Not only that, the supply of misinformation and contradictory information is pretty huge, too.

I decided that basic preparation information should be all in one place, simply explained, so you can just get on with it instead of wasting a lot of your time trying to figure out what to do. I start by throwing in a little bit about my reasons for prepping, but I'll also have real examples to explain why I feel the way I do, because I just can't help myself. Maybe you'll agree, maybe not. Then, it's on to brass tacks.

If I can, I'll recommend specific products to buy, and give you some specific places to buy them from. Some of these products I have or still plan to get, others are just examples that I've found or heard about. It's up to you to determine what to buy; I just point you in the right direction. Sometimes I direct you to the manufacturer's website, and you can find the retailer of your choice yourself. Of course, some retailers that I mention may not be operating anymore when you go to their website, but preparation is a growth industry, so if they're out of business, they must have been doing something very wrong. The products should still be available, though. I found Mountain House freeze-dried food pouches at my local Costco (at a very good price), and Sams Club, WalMart, and BJs Warehouse also carry lines of survival foods, which should tell you something about the growing popularity of prepping.

I dedicate this book to the very few people who have come up with realistic and useful information, and especially those of the Church of Jesus Christ of Latter Day Saints (the Mormons) without whom, in my opinion, we wouldn't have all the commercial enterprises that make our survival preparations as easy as a few mouse clicks. A tenet of that religion is individual preparedness, leading to a large population of consumers of preparedness supplies, which in turn created many businesses catering to that need, which are also available to the rest of us.

Introduction

So, you're interested in Prepping? What do you want to prepare for? The blizzard of the century, a solar flare, a terrorist attack, perhaps widespread crop failures, an Avian Flu or some other pandemic outbreak? Maybe a massive economic crash? The list goes on and on, because there are so many ways for things to go wrong big time. Personally, I think a terrorist attack on the power grid or the results of a huge solar flare is a greater risk than some enemy EMP (Electro Magnetic Pulse) attack, but who am I to say? My crystal ball is no better than yours. Actually, no one else has a better crystal ball than yours, and so if you think that "your" disaster scenario is more likely than "my" disaster scenario, that's perfectly okay, maybe you're more correct than I am. I hope to never find out, and I'd have to assume you don't either. Life during and after such an event will certainly not improve things! You can only prepare as much as you can and hope for the best.

No matter what happens, or even if nothing happens at all, we still need food and drink, sanitation and security. You may decide to add things like Chemical/Biological/Nuclear suits and gas masks and iodine tablets to your supplies even though I don't include them in my supplies – stupid me if you end up being right and I end up being wrong. Feel free to scavenge through my supplies when I'm gone, there's a lot of good stuff there.

What if I'm right and you're wrong? You'll have some extra gear you didn't need to use. So what? We're only trying to satisfy our own needs and wants, to make ourselves more confident that we can be self-sufficient, and take care of ourselves if we need to. Maybe we're both screwed, and only the people who are sitting in a bunker deep underground will survive. Let's hope no jealous neighbors piled a bunch of big rocks on top of their escape hatch, so at least someone will be around to start over.

This will be the only section that deals with my philosophy and motivations behind prepping. It'll also have an overview of some of the subjects I'll be dealing with, as well as some good nuggets of information that I'll throw in and may not repeat later. After this, it will all be specific "how-to" information, without a lot of "blah, blah, blah" (or as little as I can limit myself to).

I apologize in advance for not having all the answers. I say the generic word "event" a lot, because as I've said, my crystal ball is no better than yours. Take "event" to mean "whatever happens that requires us to start using our emergency supplies and other survival measures."

Even though I can bring up things you should think about and research more deeply for yourself, everyone is starting out in a different situation. Crystal ball or not, while there's a long list of events we might face, no one can know exactly what event we will face, or when it will occur (if at all). You can spend your life savings on an expensive shelter, and end up never needing it. You can spend a little extra money every week on groceries, and it might get you through an otherwise very uncomfortable month or two in the near future.

This book will guide you through starting your preparations; it's up to you to continue along the road to satisfy your individual needs and wants based on your circumstances. I'm not going to include 50 pages of recipes you can cook up with your supplies, nor am I going to do a page each about the complete life cycle and nutritional advantages of each bean in existence just to bulk up the page count of this book. If you are that interested, you can easily find that elsewhere. I did, and it's pretty boring stuff, I've got to tell you. I'm not going to teach you how to build a yurt or a teepee, or an igloo, because even though I've seen these instructions available on the web, I really don't have a clue. I'm either going to be in my own home or a nearby home in case of an event. If you think you're going to bug out to the forest somewhere, I suggest you research and learn wood crafts long before you need to use them – you may not be able to Google the instructions after an event happens.

Some of the things I bring up, I have yet to see anyone else address. I've brought up all the things I could think of that you should at least think about, and I've gathered the best of the information I've found, and I've tried to put that information into my own, hopefully simpler terms to make it more understandable. Sorry if I use too many big words. If you have a problem understanding any words, that's what dictionaries are for. Save your life and expand you mind!

So why am I a Prepper? We live in a complex, globally interconnected civilization. For most of us, at least here in the United States, life runs pretty smoothly. While there might be bumps in the road, most of us can't imagine that anything very bad, with long-term consequences, could happen to us. After all, this is America, we can get through anything. The occasional terrorist attack, a tornado, earthquake, or hurricane here and there, an early snowstorm that knocks out electricity for a week, they're just bumps in the road, nothing that will inconvenience us for more than a few days, maybe a week or so. It sucks at the time, but if needed, help is always "on the way."

Once Upon A Time, people used to hate the King when his tax collectors came around, but they also loved the King for keeping the barbarians and other enemies at bay, so they didn't come to the village and chop them up or drag them away to be slaves. The vast majority of people didn't worry about much more than having the right amount of rain for their crops so they wouldn't starve, hoped that witches didn't do them harm, that barbarians didn't show up, and who knows what else. I have no idea what beliefs they used to think of as "nuts". Maybe crazy stuff like believing the Earth was round, or that illnesses weren't caused by evil spirits.

One thing I'm certain they did not think was nuts was to prepare as best they could to get themselves through the next day, the next week, the next winter, as long a time period as they could. They could never know what the future would bring, and it usually brought bad stuff. That kind of thinking lasted for most of human history. Now, Liberals think Conservatives are nuts, Conservatives think Liberals are nuts, and most people think that anyone that thinks too much differently than they do are nuts. A lot of people think that Preppers are nuts, too. In some cases, they'd be right; every group has its nuts.

There happens to be a psychological condition, called the "Normalcy Bias," that prevents most of us from believing that anything really bad can happen to us. Look it up, Wikipedia has an interesting article. Basically, it means that to your brain, if it's never happened before, it won't ever happen. You might not believe what's occurring, even if it's happening right before your eyes! Sure, some of us have been through some horrible experiences, and have had that bias beaten out of us the hard way. Others of us have heard enough (because we've been paying attention to the news and not just the sports scores) so that we're beginning to understand that bad things can and do happen, they may end up happening to us, and suspect that expecting the cavalry to come rushing in from over the horizon to help us is not always a good bet.

I happen to think that people who believe nothing bad can ever happen are the ones who are nuts. So which kind of crazy is better, being prepared for something that may never happen or not being prepared and then something bad does happen? Which variety of nut has a better chance for survival in the admittedly teeny-weeny chance that something bad does happen to them? For any individual, it's probable that nothing bad will happen, but it's certainly possible that something bad will happen. Want to bet your life, the lives of your loved ones, when it's so easy to just be prepared?

Having a two week supply of food isn't being prepared. You can survive for a couple of weeks without food. You can't survive for a couple of months without food. Being prepared doesn't mean a specific target of time, but you have to think about what can happen and how long it would take for things to get back to normal.

To me, having worked in the power industry for many years, based on what I know about how long it takes to manufacture certain equipment and how long it'll take to install that equipment, the time we can be without power due to a widespread enough disaster, can actually range from 3 months to a year, even more! It's normally less, much less, because there's enough manpower and spare equipment available to take care of any localized outage. Is it probable that any area can be without power for 6 months? Honestly, the answer is no. Is it possible? Of course it's possible. It's certainly not impossible. It's a lot more possible than us being hit by an asteroid. It might actually be somewhat less possible than being hit with a worldwide pandemic of a new strain of influenza or some other disease. When people say "it can't happen", it's usually just an ignorant way of saying "it can't happen again", which is both obviously and logically false.

"There's no way a major volcanic eruption can affect the climate so much that almost the whole world will not be able to grow food for a year!" That may sound reasonable, but it's a lie. "There's no way there could be a disease that spreads so fast and is so deadly that it will kill off a significant fraction of the population!" Another lie. Unfortunately, "There's no way an asteroid can hit the Earth and kill off almost all life" is yet another lie. I don't think anyone can or would want to be prepared for that last one, which may not happen again for millions of years anyway, but it's well within our means to be prepared for the first two, both of which happened within the last couple of centuries.

I can't understand why anyone would be against prepping. I also can't understand why people would be ignorant enough not to want to be prepared.

There's no physical pain involved in prepping, and mentally, it can only increase your confidence and peace of mind. You don't have to shave your head, or dye your hair pink, or pierce your nose (but no one will stop you if that's what you really want to do). You don't have to swear allegiance to some goofy guru, you don't even need to join a club. There's no required reading list aside from researching what you want to know, and there are no tests (except there may be one heck of a surprise final exam!) You don't have to waste time going to meetings every Saturday morning. You don't even have to wear a funny hat.

Basically, Prepping is just getting "stuff"! People get stuff all the time. You just need to get the right stuff.

You can't eat that big screen TV, or your car, or that bracelet or ring. You do need to get something to eat, but you don't know right now when you'll need to eat that particular food, nor what the conditions will be at the time, so you need to get food that won't need refrigeration, is easy to prepare, and will last a long time. It can be bland, boring food, but it can also be delicious food. You get to pick, based on your tastes and budget. It's the same with stuff to drink.

Getting stuff to eat, getting stuff to drink, and making sure you get to keep that stuff if it's ever needed, that's the basic idea. That's prepping!

The End.

Thanks for stopping by.

Only kidding. You start there, and you can stop at any time. You don't have to have an arsenal. You don't have to dig a 50 foot deep lead lined bunker in your backyard. You don't have to carry a gas mask with you 24/7. You don't need to join the 0.01% of the extreme Preppers they do TV shows about. Just get stuff to eat and stuff to drink, and some simple equipment.

Stay low-profile and reasonable about it. Don't empty your bank account or mortgage your house. That way, there's no risk of being institutionalized, and no one will confiscate your estate due to mental incompetence. You may not need any of your stuff for months, years, or decades, if ever. It's just a hobby. It hurts no one. It can help people someday. It can save lives! There's nothing evil about it – it's all good. You're not taking food off your families table, either – you're putting food ON your families table, when they'll need it most. Be ready for almost anything, and you'll be very happy if something does happen. Even if you go to your grave having never had to survive a major event, at least you had one less thing to worry about while you were here. Sure, there are people who aren't ready for anything, and they never worry either. Maybe their own lives don't have much value to them, who knows? There are people who take stupid risks all the time.

Maybe sometime in the future, you will hear people tell you that they have nothing to worry about because nothing bad will happen, so they don't need to store any food, and you will feel bad for them; because you fear that their brand of nuttiness might kill them slowly and horribly someday.

Human Nature

More and more of us have been keeping our eyes open, we have seen human nature at work, and we're beginning to understand that our civilization is really pretty fragile. You may have heard the term "the veneer of civilization". Veneer is a very thin coating, making something look good, but it's just on the surface. Thankfully, part of our veneer is called "the thin blue line". You may have heard that term. If you haven't, I suggest you Google it. It's a very thin line, indeed. It really is only designed to work if things are relatively "normal". Anyway, the reality is sinking in, and we're not all that confident that everything that can go wrong will always be made right quickly.

The home team wins a ball game, and so-called "fans" riot in the streets, burning and looting. A crowd is waiting in line to buy the newest hot toy or electronic gadget, and people are actually crushed to death by the mob. The merest indication that law enforcement cannot contain an outbreak of civil unrest and all the scum join in. Our society has degenerated to the point that law enforcement tends to stand by, letting the vermin have their way. "It's only property damage, no sense in anyone getting hurt." Which translates to "let them do what they want to each other, no sense in us hurting any of these vermin, they'll end up suing us!" The mob in Greece is disturbed that they may no longer get to retire at 50, so they riot and burn down a government building – an occupied building. People died. Remember Rodney King? When the rioting started in Los Angeles, the police all ran the other way. People died, buildings burned. But it was "contained." Of course, for days it was too dangerous for the decent people to risk leaving their homes. It was too dangerous for the police! It would have been a waste of time to risk going to the market anyway, they were already looted or burned.

When disasters happen in a small area, sure, it's reasonable to expect help from the outside. What happens if the "event" happens to be widespread, affecting more area than the usual emergency response can handle? FEMA might have a big budget, but they can't be everywhere at once. If you're in an area that tops the response list, some kind of help is probably on the way. If you're on the bottom of the list, you can be patient and suffer – but you're on your own. If things get bad enough that even the emergency responders decide that they must look out for their own loved ones first and foremost, who's coming to help you?

Unless you are living in a cave, you will have heard all the news stories over the years about how, whenever a hurricane is on the way, for those who don't evacuate the immediate coastline, the target area's supermarkets are stripped bare for many miles around. People stock up on anything and everything they can get their hands on; because they know that the stores will be closed, or at least mostly empty, for a while.

Whether they recognize it or not, these people are Preppers. It might only be for the short term, but the idea is the same. They know something bad is on the way, supplies will be hard if not impossible to get, so they get what they feel they'll need in advance. Unfortunately, most people only become Preppers when the event is clearly known in advance. They can't escape the knowledge that the situation is real and imminent, and they need to prepare as best they can.

A growing number of us are coming to the understanding that not all events are so clearly defined, nor as easily predicted as a hurricane on the way. Yes, sometimes the "events" are sure things. Nowadays, we're all informed in advance that a hurricane is coming. We know almost to the hour when, and we also know pretty close to where it'll make landfall. In 1938, they didn't know. A hurricane hit New England, and over 600 people died.

I admit there's not much you can do to prepare for a storm surge, other than having a "bug out" bag and running away in a timely manner. These days, it's pretty certain you'll have sufficient warning. I think by now, we've got hurricanes licked. Similarly with Tsunamis, we're working on that. After a quarter of a million people died in the last big one, many areas of the world now get at least some warning, and the smart people drop everything and run to high ground. A major winter blizzard warning usually gives you at least a day or two to join the mob at the supermarket. There's usually time enough to be a Prepper when the media tells you to be one.

Unfortunately, other events can come without any warning. It may be weather related, it may not. Any breakdown in the day to day working of society, even to the extent of a breakdown of the social order, can be considered an event. Even if there is advanced warning, or a build-up to the event, there may not be time to stockpile all the survival supplies you'll need or want, especially if you're ordering online, and waiting for a delivery from halfway across the country. You need to start now, and continue until you are satisfied.

For most people, if they aren't told exactly what will happen, or when it'll happen, they don't worry too much about taking any extraordinary precautions, or even simple and obvious precautions. A few candles, extra batteries, a case of beer and a couple of bags of chips might be minimal but sufficient preparation for being stuck in the house for a couple of days, but even then, they'll only prepare when the nightly newscast tells them they should. That's a problem. Time may be against them. They think that if they don't know exactly what they're preparing for, they won't know what they'll need. People throw up their hands and say "why bother?" That goes well with "nothing's going to happen anyway."

"Why bother?" and "nothing's going to happen anyway!" is the perfect recipe for becoming a helpless victim. How self-reliant is that? Bad question. The idea of self-reliance has been slowly stripped away from our nation, to be replaced by reliance on authority. How about you? Do you have small children depending on you for their comfort and survival? Children are not going to be impressed by you bitching about how worthless FEMA is if they're cold, hungry, and scared. They'll be looking at you, and hopefully they won't be able to figure out that in fact, their own parents are losers who can't feed them dinner (because said parents decided that they don't need to worry, if times get tough, some strangers from the government will be coming to take care of them all.)

You might be pretty comfortable for a week, or two, or three. What happens if week 4 rolls around? What happens if you're in your second month of not being able to get any more food, maybe the water isn't coming out of your taps anymore, and the FEMA trucks haven't rolled into town yet?

Will you go begging from your neighbors who are probably in the same shape you're in? Maybe you will, if you know one of your acquaintances or neighbors are Preppers – you know, the ones you thought were nuts, because nothing will happen? Maybe they'll share. Maybe they won't. Want to bet your life, and the life of your family on it? Oh, you've got a gun? You'll make them share? They almost certainly have guns, too. Ever been in a shootout?

The fact is, no matter what could possibly happen, there are basic supplies that everyone should have to get them through a reasonable length of time, and that's why I've written this. You don't need to spend a lot of money on stuff that will rot in your basement or in a closet, never to be used if nothing at all ever happens. You'll use almost all of it, you'll just have a lot of extra stuff stocked up at any one time.

For example, how long will your toilet tissue last? Go count – really! You have a six pack? A 24 pack? Do you just pick up a couple of rolls a week? What if you can't get any more for three months? Six months? No paper towels, no facial tissues, no cheating. You pick the timeframe you are comfortable being supplied for. Let's say you pick 3 months. Wouldn't it be prudent to keep 3 months' worth of toilet tissue, plus a couple of extra rolls just in case? You'd replace it as you use it just like now, but you will already have built up an emergency reserve in case the supply runs dry for whatever reason. Don't forget to keep it in a watertight plastic bag if there's any chance it can get wet – wet TP means no TP. Those plastic storage bags you suck the air out of with a vacuum cleaner works great for the purpose.

For those old enough to remember, in December 1973, Johnny Carson, the hugely popular host of the Tonight Show, mentioned (in jest) that because of a huge government order for the stuff, there was a big toilet paper shortage coming. By noon the next day, just about every roll of toilet paper on every store shelf in the whole country was bought. Really! Stores could not keep TP in stock, as every roll was bought as soon as they tried restocking the shelves! Even a couple of days later, when Johnny explained on his show that he was just kidding, people still bought up and horded toilet paper for the next 3 weeks! What if you were down to your last roll, didn't watch Johnny

Carson, and went shopping – only to find out there was no toilet paper to be had? Anywhere! For days! Based on a joke?

More and more people are deciding that we will be responsible for ourselves, and not wait around like sheep for some outside agency to come and bail us out. No matter what the event may be, we have determined that we will be prepared for anything we can, to the extent that we can. We are Preppers. It's just a harmless hobby that could end up saving our lives, that's all.

I'm not preparing for the "Zombie Apocalypse" (although that sounds good on TV). I'd imagine that very few people, if any, seriously believe that the Undead will be walking the earth, looking to eat our brains. Actually, when the term comes up, it really means the starving masses wandering to find whatever food they can get, any way they can get it. That will be, sadly, the huge majority of the population.

I'm also not preparing for a massive nuclear attack. If that is the case, I will put my head between my legs, and kiss my butt goodbye. I don't want to survive an event where "the living will envy the dead!" That's a little too much excitement, everyone has a limit. Maybe 20 years ago, but not at my age.

What I do want to do is make it through any extended period of "bad days" in as much safety and comfort as I can, to hopefully join with other survivors to reminisce about the hard times, like our grandparents or great-grandparents did about the Great Depression. The only two problems we have are, when will the "bad days" arrive, and how long will they last? Are we talking a month, 3 months, 6 months or more? I wish I knew. It would make prepping so much easier.

The reality is that most people don't have more than a one week supply of food at home. One fully stocked week. If the markets are empty, they may stretch it to two, but by week three, the milk and bread are long gone, the couple of cans of crappy soup no one in the family likes, the last couple of cans of beans, maybe the last box of spaghetti on the shelf will have been eaten and then what will they do? Anyone see those FEMA trucks yet?

Unless you're Amish, you live in a civilization that over many decades has been built around the use of electricity. We are all dependent on electricity, and even the Amish buy supplies that someone else needed electricity to create in some way. If you've ever been without electricity for more than a few hours, you know what a hardship the lack of it causes. By now, many of us have been without it for a day, even a week at a time. Fortunately, power outages are generally local or regional, and repairs proceed, sometimes with additional crews called in from outside the area. Generally, the problem is a storm that takes down trees, which in turn take power lines down, rather than the destruction of very expensive and hard to replace equipment like transformers (although that occasionally happens, too).

I'm preparing for the power to be out for several weeks, maybe even several months or more (maybe a lot more – some major electrical equipment can take weeks, months, or even a year or more to replace); or a food shortage (a lack of electricity or fuel for delivery trucks WILL lead to food shortages); or a lack of municipal water (another potential result of a long-term lack of electricity) for however long it lasts, within reason. As I've said, I'm not getting ready for "the end of the world as we know it." Few can. Just because some storage food will last for 20 years doesn't mean it's practical or even possible to store a 20 year supply of it! If "TEOTWAWKI" (The End Of The World As We Know It) ever really does happen, guess what? Don't worry about it, it's rather simple. Our fate is pre-ordained – if we survive, we're going to be farm labor. Unless you have some specific craft-type skill so that people will be willing to trade you food for your labor, you get to do "the job that no American wants to do" – the job that 80-90% or more of Americans used to do. I don't want to farm, but I do like to eat. I can pick crops like any migrant farmworker if I absolutely had to (okay, a lot slower, for sure). Will work for food, you know. My back won't like it, but what can you do?

I want to be ready for pretty much just the mundane events that could end up being life threatening if you can't just go get a motel room in the next town or even the next state, and heading for your brother-in-law's place to freeload won't do you any good because they'll be in the same boat you are.

Once again, to those who don't believe it can happen, in Feb. 1998, Auckland, New Zealand had a 66 day blackout due to power cable failure. It only affected a few thousand people, but they suffered for a little over 2 months without power! In 1965, 30 million people were without power in the Northeast US due to problems with the power grid. In August of 2003, more than 50 million people were without power on the US East Coast. Those blackouts didn't last very long, but what if they did? Very little of the electrical infrastructure was actually damaged, but the safeguards worked – all the power was shut down. It took most of the time to carefully bring the power back online without causing more damage. The more equipment that gets damaged, the longer it will take to restore power.

The power grid is a huge, complex, interconnected machine, yet it is fairly fragile. It's mostly above ground. It can, and has been affected by natural causes such as weather, solar flares, and mechanical breakdowns. So far, we haven't seen terrorism, EMP (Electro Magnetic Pulse), or cyber-attack on the grid, although they have the potential to cause great damage. Small parts can fail, large parts can fail. Failures can be restored in hours, days, or weeks, but it is possible it could even take months, or more. It all depends on what goes wrong, and how much goes wrong at the same time.

You might have an emergency generator. Great! That will get you through a couple of days, maybe a week or two. How much fuel do you have on hand? Will you be able to get more? There are very expensive generators that are hooked up to natural gas, others that will feed off your very large tank of propane. If that is the case, good for you. You'll be the envy of the neighborhood. I'll discuss more about envious neighbors later.

What if you couldn't drive far enough to find temporary accommodations until whatever happened blows over? Keep in mind, the more people affected, the more people are competing to find those motel and hotel rooms. Places will be filled up farther and farther away from wherever you are.

I'm sticking to the theory (or hope) that things will get back to normal even if it takes a year. I'm too old to want to start life again as a farmer (although needs must when the devil drives), and even though I live in a small town, it's still in the Northeast, midway between New York and Boston. Some Preppers would think me suicidal!

We all can't move to Kansas, or Idaho, or Utah, or wherever, to be in a small town surrounded by lots and lots of farmland, far from any major cities, which would be the ideal, defensible community. Well, some of us could, but that's a bit extreme, especially if your job doesn't allow you to telecommute. Trying to do it after the event begins won't work out too well, either, with all the competition and perhaps difficulty in travel and obtaining mortgage money, and need I say "etc." You may not have to worry about your job anymore, but it'll be hell finding and buying a place if it has already hit the fan. Besides, I don't want to leave my friends and family behind, and they'd have a problem running to the middle of nowhere "just in case" too, I'd bet anything on it.

If you are lucky enough to have the finances to be able to do that, to invest a lot of money to reserve a place to bug-out to, just in case, there are opportunities for you to do that. Aside from picking a small town somewhere and buying a little farm, there are groups attempting to create purpose-built communities that are just the thing. Here's one I know nothing more about than their website, although it's a compelling idea (and they've got some great articles to read on their website): www.codegreenprep.com

The big problem with this idea is that unless you move there full time, you'll have to be able to get to your bug-out destination if the time ever comes. You'll also need time to get to know and be accepted by the neighbors. You'll have to have it well stocked in advance, in case you do have to go there after a major event (unless you can make it there with a big truckload of supplies). You may end up having to defend your property there just as much as wherever you're leaving from. Granted, the population density will be a lot lower, but that may also make your place a more inviting, out of the way target for looters. Well, enough about that, the internet is filled with thousands of hours of reading about the subject, and I'd like to stick to pontificating about my game plan.

I have to say once again, sadly, our society has become so totally screwed-up that wanting to be self-sufficient is seen as an aberration. It didn't used to be this way. People used to strive to have reserves for tough times, knowing that survival may be up to them. Tough times used to happen with frightening regularity. Now, dependency on the government to come and fix things no matter what happens is so ingrained into the masses that anything that smacks of having "little faith" in "big government" is considered crazy, which is just the way the politicians want it to be!

"Nothing will happen, and even if something does happen, we will be taken care of." Does that sound irrational to you? Maybe not, if you've never heard of Hurricane Katrina.

The media, negative scum that they are, pick out the most extreme amongst the Prepper movement, and create the illusion that being prepared is crazy. Certainly there are some Preppers who overdo it – or do they? Either way, the damage is done. So much so, that many Preppers keep it to themselves.

One reason for secrecy, which many websites warn people about, is the idea that if the neighbors know, they will expect you to help them if the time ever comes, or even that they will come and take your supplies if they're ever needed. These websites, and many Preppers, are adamant about people keeping their preps a secret. In my case, that's why I want a LOT of supplies - I actually WANT to help the neighbors – I'll need their eyes and ears, if not their guns. If my supply is also their supply, I guess they'll have to help me protect it whether they want to or not. How's that for logic? It's my logic, and there will be only one way to find out if I'm right.

There are great arguments for secrecy, but I don't think secrecy will hold for the long term. Sure, if there's no event, no one would ever care what you've got stashed away in your basement. Even if the neighbors find out what you're up to, they might think you're strange, or paranoid, but they'd have no reason to actually bother you. After an event, since they'll know you're prepared, they'll look to you for salvation, but it'll be harder and harder to maintain secrecy anyway, especially if you're in a suburban area where your neighbors are close.

In an event, with nothing else to do all day but to congregate together and speculate on the situation, the neighbors will be suspicious every time you excuse yourself to try to secretly go cook up a meal, especially as time goes on and they're getting hungrier and hungrier – but you're not. If you have children, are you going to keep them locked up indoors indefinitely? If not, are they going to keep the secret from their hungry friends? Aren't they going to want to help their friends?

Think about it. Are you and your family going to be virtual shut-ins, never leaving your house or opening your door? Never showing a light at night? I'm sure at some point some of your neighbors are going to be nice enough to come by to check on you to see if you're okay. They won't have much else to do, will they? If you don't answer the door, make like you're gone, in just a matter of days, your house is going to be checked to see what food is in your cupboards. If you do answer the door, they'll know you're home. Will they then leave you alone, to perhaps starve (not knowing how prepared you are? Will you at some point have to come out to seek water? I just don't believe in the secrecy aspect. I don't think it's possible. Your energy will be better spent on trying to convince some neighbors to stock up before an event occurs. Of course, this is based on the lifestyle of the suburbs.

On the other hand, in an urban area, I think secrecy is very important. That's where the risk to life and limb goes up sharply. No one could possibly store enough food to feed the whole block for a week, if even a day. Urban areas are where people are most concentrated, and where food stores require constant resupply - there's simply no way they can stock enough food to handle the large quantity of customers they serve for more than a few days, a week at most. A lot more people will get hungry in a small area a lot sooner.

Also, in the event of a serious economic emergency (or any event that causes one), consider the large number of people who are not going to appreciate any interruption in the well-oiled redistribution of wealth routine that they have grown dependent on. A lot of them will try to take care of that redistribution all by themselves. What choice will they have? The only good news is that they probably don't have a lot of money for arms and ammunition.

The bad news is, also consider that although studies vary, one study reports that there are now over 900,000 presumably armed gang-bangers nationwide. They're concentrated in the big cities. Fighting each other over drug territory will rapidly change to foraging and fighting for food – fighting anyone! Right now, they mostly bother each other, with the unfortunate occasional collateral damage to the neighborhood children. Gangsters have parents and children and siblings to feed, too. They DO have the money for arms and ammunition, and experience using them. They don't hesitate to kill each other, and they won't hesitate to kill you.

I can't give much advice for those of you living in a very rural area. You're probably pretty self-sufficient already, but you'd better have some plans made with the neighbors for security, just in case. If you are isolated, you are also a tempting target of those folks I've already spoken about, if they ever make it to your area.

Another sad reason for secrecy is that people think that if it's found out that they are Preppers, they'll be considered nuts. I found out that at work, just in my little department, four of us are Preppers. It wasn't easy, no one just announced it, and you have to kind of dance around the subject before people open up. It's sad, because we have so much to learn from each other. No one knows it all, or where to get the best supplies for the money, or even what supplies to get. Not only that, in groups, you can get quantity discounts on supplies from some vendors. Recently, three of us split a case of canned butter from New Zealand. Real butter in cans! Shelf life measured in years! You see, you can't fry with powdered butter, and cooking reconstituted eggs are going to be better with butter. I never knew about canned butter, it's not available at any supermarket I've ever been to.

Secrecy? I have a different idea. For one thing, I don't give a crap what people think of me. If you want to think I'm nuts for not wanting to depend on the government to save me, assuming that they even can (which remains to be proven), feel free. I lose nothing, because if you think of the government as your keeper, you're one of the people I detest anyway. However, I think it's a duty to evangelize others to the prepping way of thinking. The more of us who are prepared, the more who can band together and protect what we've got, the fewer of us will end up as dependents, and beggars, with our hands out and our stomachs empty if the time ever comes. If nothing ever happens in our lifetime, we'll still have lots of neat stuff, especially for camping trips, and we haven't hurt anyone, have we?

Speaking of "hands out and stomachs empty," most decent people want to help others who really need help. I know I do. It's a very tiny minority who will actually risk their own safety to do so. I've been a police officer, and I've been in the military. As they say, "Been there, done that." If I have enough food stored so that I can eat for three months if the need arises, that will only provide one day of food for a mob of 90 people. If I distribute all my food, what will I do the next day? I'll be just one more of the hungry mob with my hands out. Nah, not me. I paid my dues. I think I'd rather survive. Will I feel bad, eating well, knowing people out there are hungry? Hell, people are hungry right now, all over the world. I can't fix it, so I don't dwell on it. What happens if these hungry people are wandering the streets by my home, looking for a meal? What if they find out I've got food, and they're banging on my door, demanding that I share? That's a moral dilemma. What does one do, distribute food, or bullets?

If an event lasts for more than a few weeks, there will be an awful lot of hungry people who will be getting increasingly desperate. I can tell you with certainty that under those circumstances, it may do no good to call the police if a bunch of people decide that if you have food, you have to share it with them whether you want to or not. If the police, by then, aren't home protecting their own families, they may well be out among the hungry mob themselves, especially if they have families to feed too. This brings us to another fact that makes the average citizen cringe – you must have the means, the fortitude, and hopefully some training, to be able to defend what you've got. Crazy Preppers indeed!

If I were the one starving, maybe with a family at home starving, I'd be a man with nothing to lose, wouldn't I? If I found out that you have food, and I've got to get some food, I would certainly appreciate it if you gave me some, but I really wouldn't be in a position to take no for an answer (unless you can MAKE me take no for an answer). If you give me some food today, I'll know where to go tomorrow, won't I? Multiply me times everyone who isn't prepared – do you get the picture?

Of course, even if you're not willing to defend what is yours, you should still stock up, you might be lucky enough to have neighbors or friends who will take care of the defending as long as you take care of the feeding. It would be good to solidify an arrangement like that in advance, though.

Family

Another point I want you to think about is the fact that just because you decide to be a Prepper, that may be big news to the rest of your family, the people you live with. They're going to be affected by your new hobby. You may be able to sneak it up on them, but eventually they'll notice all the extra stuff. I'd hope that they will respect you enough to let you do your thing, and it would be great if they can be included, especially in meal choices, etc. Of course you're going to be involving them anyway, even if they don't choose to participate. You're hardly going to be able to stock up for yourself and not share with them if the time comes, are you?

The more involvement the family has in the process of preparing, the better off you'll all be. You don't want to scare the kids with stories of the end of the world, but hopefully they've been through a power outage by now, and that is an angle you need to play on. It's "The power goes out from time to time, cause stuff breaks, so we want to be able to do whatever we want even if the power is out", not "the terrorists may succeed in frying the electric grid and we may never have electricity ever again". The kids only need to know that you need lights if the power goes out, you need to cook food if the power (or even the gas) goes out, and you need food that you don't have to refrigerate or freeze if the power goes out.

If you are truly one of the "edgier" of us, like to the tune of digging that 50 foot deep bunker, I don't know how you're going to do this, but try not to inflict your worst fears on the kids – shoulder that burden on your own! After all, "What if the power is out for a couple of weeks?" is a reasonable excuse to kick off prepping. "The power may go off and never come back, ever" is way over the top. You may believe it, it may even eventually go down like that, but can you please throttle it down for the kids?

If you come at them all "The End of the World is Coming!", if you make them think you went nuts, you may sour them from participating from the get-go. Or cause them psychological problems. Eventually, supplies for a month can grow into three, six, before you know it you'll be up to a year or more, but CRAWL before you WALK, and WALK before you RUN!

Just because some people are not doing anything to prepare, there's no way that you and your family are going to suffer any inconvenience just because other people aren't smart enough to be prepared. That's your story, and stick to it.

There's no need to give the kids nightmares about zombies coming to get them, or even stories to tell their friends at school. They may eventually figure things out for themselves, but remember, crawl, walk, run! Don't scare the children, just teach them what self-sufficiency is all about by example.

If you plan on bugging out, you can have them help with putting together their bug out bags, include their favorite treats (snacks and juice boxes, etc.) and occasionally drill the "big escape". Maybe head to a park, pitch a tent, and turn a drill into a fun weekend adventure.

If you're bugging in, have the occasional meal from the supply shelves. I suggest doing what I do with non-Preppers, I start with a "taste test" of freeze dried meals, so you can find out what they like and what they won't eat. Even if you're going to stock up on mostly canned goods or bulk stuff, there's no excitement in a dinner of Chef Boyardee canned spaghetti and meatballs or Chunky Soup. Go for an assortment of Mountain House pouches, like Lasagna, Turkey Tetrazini, stuff like that. It should be pretty exotic to people who've never had freeze dried meals before.

Then you can do a "blackout day", where you do breakfast, lunch, and dinner, and go through the whole day with no electricity, just to see what it's like. I realize this might mean civil war if there's no TV, computer, or internet use. You can always have music playing on a battery or wind up radio. The little ones will probably get a kick out of it, and except if you're one of the (for no good reason, in my opinion) super secretive types, you can and should let any adolescents share the event with a friend. Believe me, it may have been decades since my teens, but I still remember. No matter what hardship you impose on them at that age, if they're able to have their best friend there to share it with them, it'll be so much better for everyone involved. Of course, if you have teens and they're into it for its own sake, friends or not, you're golden. The idea is that you want them, and yourself, to have a taste of what surviving will be like before there may be no choice. Ease into it, make it fun. There may be plenty of time, if you ever have to do it for real, for it to become drudgery.

As there's not much the rest of the family has to DO aside from not taking up your supply storage space with their stuff, at least at first, the biggest obstacle may be a spouse who doesn't want to see all that money making its way onto shelves in the basement. Hopefully, if the rational argument about how it's insurance against risk doesn't work, there's also the strictly financial argument based on the ever increasing cost of food. That'll work for a small stockpile, but in time, the five gallon pails of rice and beans may require some convincing, and then there's that equipment for cooking, heating, water purification, etc. Hopefully you guys will be able to grow into it together. You're only doing it for the good of your family, after all.

If someone can't see that it's a good idea to have a way to heat the house or cook food (or even have food) if the power is out, I'm sorry. Hopefully you haven't added to the gene pool yet. Perhaps your spouse has a hobby of his or her own that soaks up a bit of money regularly? Isn't it only fair that you do too? If their hobby is collecting firearms and shooting at the range, congratulations, you've got it made, you're halfway there. Adding storage food to a household with guns is a lot easier than adding guns to a stockpile of food. I'll get more into that later on.

Random Grumbling

Mother Nature has given us a taste of what can happen more than once in the past.

"Back in April of 1815, Mount Tambora in Indonesia created the largest volcanic eruption in recorded history. The estimated 800 megaton explosion killed at least 71,000 – and possibly hundreds of thousands more (if not millions) due to the chaotic climactic shifts that followed. More than 400 million tons of sulfuric gases were ejected into the atmosphere, leading to the often-cited "Year Without a Summer" in North America and Europe. Crops failed, livestock died, and heavy snows in the U.S. fell well into July. In other words, it was a terrible event – and one that may be poised to happen again"

www.ecorazzi.com/2011/09/20/worlds-deadliest-volcano-missing-summer/

This may not happen again for a hundred, or a thousand years. Maybe it'll happen the year after next. If a climate event ever occurs again such that we miss a growing season over a large enough area of the world, there's going to be a food shortage of historic proportions. Little food available for a whole year! But that could never really happen again, right?

I know I keep harping on this, but we depend on electricity for our modern world to function. Loss of the electric grid for an extended time will profoundly affect every aspect of modern life. A really severe solar flare has the ability to knock out the bulk of the electrical grid anywhere in the world. It's already happened, locally, in several places, and it could happen again big time. The grid could be badly damaged by a totally unexpected and unprecedented cyber-attack. Experts have been warning for years that the grid is not hardened against these kinds of events. The electric grid contains many complex and expensive parts that are actually quite sensitive.

There are only so many spares available, and nowhere near enough to replace the bulk of our grid in any reasonable amount of time. The really big transformers, the ones that move the bulk power from the power plants around the country, are such monster machines that only about 100 of them are manufactured each year, worldwide, they cost millions of dollars each, and they take around 2 ½ to 3 years from the time they're ordered to the time they arrive where needed. They're as

big as a house! There are a couple of thousands of them in the USA. If even a few hundred of them require replacement, there are going to be wide areas of the country that just won't have power for a long time. It's as simple as that. The number of spares in the whole country is very limited. We don't even make them here. They're made in Asia and South America. Not only would they have to be manufactured, they also have to be shipped.

Then there are the tens of thousands of smaller transformers, also not in great supply. These are not parts that are sitting on store shelves. Utility companies know how many they replace in normal years, and the number of spares on hand are only enough to meet the need for normal circumstances, not large scale breakdowns. Not necessarily the "end of life as we know it," but we could certainly see many months, perhaps years without large portions of the electric grid operating. Generators will fly off the shelves like toilet paper in 1973, but there'll never be enough of them. Will there even be enough fuel for them, and for how long? There are too many ways for it to go wrong, each way multiplying the odds of an event actually happening. Unfortunately, with the mindset "it's not going to happen because it hasn't happened before", the risks to the grid are not being addressed with the amount of money that is required for certain prevention.

FEMA recommends that everyone keeps three days' worth of food and water. That's, of course, with the understanding that help is on the way, but it could take them a couple of days to get things organized. I have faith in the government – faith that most of what the government touches turns into an expensive boondoggle, faith that they get it wrong much more often than they get it right, and faith that above all else, they don't want to unnecessarily panic people. It's the government's faith in itself that leads to this pathetically inadequate advice. They'd like you to think they can get help to anyone, anywhere, in just a couple of days. It seems like it didn't work out too well for the folks on the Gulf Coast following Katrina. Blame and recriminations followed, but that didn't quench anyone's thirst or fill any bellies.

Personally, I think it's a reasonable and prudent idea to be able to survive for up to a year without adding anything but water to your supplies. The most consistent figure I've seen is one gallon per day per person is needed. You may or may not be able to grow some food (during the summer), but you'd certainly better be able to find and purify enough water. You'll have a hard if not impossible task to store all you'll need. You'd need at least 3,000 pounds, or 365 gallons of water to get just one person through a year (and that's just for consumption) – how many people are able to install a 500 or 1,000, or even a 5,000 gallon water tank in their backyard? How many millions of people don't even have a backyard? Can you picture, say New York City, with millions of people, fetching millions of gallons of water from the Hudson and East River every day, and purifying it!

I can't, because, luckily for NYC, the tap water comes from upstate with the help of gravity, although pumps are still needed to get the water up to all those high-rises. Most people there might never have the tap water shut off, as long as it keeps raining upstate. The city might not completely fall apart – as long as the sewage system still works. Electric pumps and motors are used for that, too. I'm sure the city has backup generators and that they have stored days and days' worth of diesel fuel, so the pumps will run for quite a while. The day they quit will be like a science fiction movie, though. I may be wrong. There might be a way for them to bypass treatment and dump all that sewage straight into the rivers. Either way, I wouldn't want to be there. Then again, it'll be great to have water, and be able to flush the toilets, but a month without food and it won't really matter if the faucets and toilets work.

Keep that anecdote in mind no matter where you live. Everyone has indoor plumbing these days. Ever think about what your toilet is connected to? Is it the city sewer system, or your own septic system?

Did you say septic system? You're a big winner! Did you say city sewer? Ever wonder what happens if it backs up? Maybe you've even heard about what happens when the sewer system reverses due to some failure or overload? I have. I've seen it on the news. I've seen people whose basements got filled with sewage due to a problem with the system. It doesn't happen, normally, but we're not talking about normal. You can bet that if the system goes kaput, I'm going to have planned a way to seal my pipes. As all the sinks and toilets in the house all lead to the same place, if worse comes to worse, I'll go down to the basement and sever and block my link to the system somehow. This isn't the kind of thing you can practice, and it would probably be prudent to have a plumber come in and install a valve (and maybe that'll make my "to do" list one of these days,) but I'll try to cap the pipe coming into my house, even if I have to fill the outlet pipe with concrete! To think that I didn't like having a septic system at my last house.

Fortunately, as long as you live reasonably close to a natural water supply (by that, I mean walking distance,) you can easily be prepared to purify hundreds if not thousands of gallons of water, and I'll explain how. If you don't live anywhere near a water supply, maybe it rains a lot? You'd better be able to set up as much rainwater scavenging as you can. You'd probably better get educated in Bugging Out, though, because when your stored water is gone, unless you live in the Pacific Northwest, I can't imagine collecting enough rainwater to make a go of it. If things don't settle down and start getting back to normal by the time you're left with just enough water to transport (which is only going to be 20 or 30 gallons unless you have a decent truck) you're going to have to go to where the water is!

While I'm strongly against starting off by purchasing a huge multi-thousand dollar food package that all survival food companies sell, you may eventually decide to do just that (after you've tried a sampling of almost everything that would be in the package, not just the free sample that some companies will send you.) You can, if you're smart about it, accumulate a years' worth of food that will store just fine for years if not decades, do it piecemeal (a little at a time for those of you in Loma Linda) and not have to spend more than an average of $4, $5, or $6 a day per person, much less if you're into cooking – bulk grains, rice, and beans are very inexpensive. Add to that a reasonable proportion of freeze dried meats, vegetables, fruits, and some treats (definitely some treats,) and you might get away with as little as $1,500 to $2,000 per person for a one year supply if you want to be frugal. How much did your last TV cost? How many meals out do you have in a year and what does that cost?

Based on how I'm doing it, taking the gourmet route, it's running me probably an average of at least $7 or $8 per day. I'll end up investing close to $3,000 to have a full year of food (and then probably add at least $1,000 more, to feed the neighbors, mooching relatives, etc.), not to mention a few hundred dollars more for equipment. By the time I'm done, I'll probably have invested something like $5,000, but that should get me through a whole year, even if I was sealed in a bubble (with river access, of course.) I started dipping my toes into this Prepping thing a couple of years ago, in 2010. I'm not done yet. If the country can manage to hold together for a couple more years, I should be all set.

It would be easy to get into the mindset that you've got to hurry up; the end could come tomorrow, take out a loan and buy everything right now! Especially if there's a food package salesman talking to you. I don't know. Paranoia - that's a good way to be taken in by a slick salesman and end up with a pallet of expensive crap that won't feed you for half the time you've paid for. You can jump right in, find yourself with a basement or garage or spare room full of stuff (which cost you a lot of money,) and then find out over the following year as you try out what you've got and research and learn more, that you've got a huge pile of crap.

My biggest mistake so far is that I bought a superwhamadyne "burns any liquid fuel" camping stove that cost me around $150, only later to find a great wood burning jet-stove that only cost about $75, and also a kerosene stove that cost about $100. My mistake was that once I started stocking up on freeze dried food, I knew I'd need to boil water, and I hadn't spent much time, at that point, doing any research on cooking equipment. Maybe someday I will sell the camping stove to someone who's planning to bug out, or use it as trade goods.

If the "event" happens tomorrow, fortunately at this point, I'm good for a several months. If it's next year, I'll be farther along. In a couple of years, I'll be ready for anything. If nothing ever happens, I know I'll be able to supplement my retirement meals with food I've already paid for, for a while, even if social security goes the way of the gold standard. Thanks to a great sale on toilet paper, I'm good on that for a couple of years! I've got over 80 rolls that I stacked inside one of those big vacuum storage bags, sucked the air out, and stashed down in the basement. I'll probably put up a second bag the next time my favorite brand is on sale. TP would make for excellent trade goods, as well.

Many of the product suggestions I'll have for you need the internet. If you don't want to buy things over the internet, don't worry. All reputable companies that sell on the internet will have a phone number available. I wouldn't list them if they didn't have a phone number and a physical address; some even do catalog sales through the mail. You can always call them to place your order, and it you want to pay by check or money order, they'll be happy to help you. If they don't, move on to a competitor. If you're not on the internet, you can go to most public libraries to get online. If you don't know how, find a relative or a neighbor kid to help you. Don't let their smugness put you off, someday there may not be an internet, and they might show up at your door begging a meal for them and their family, who bought all the latest computers, smart phones, tablets, and every other new gadget, but neglected to stock up on food in case all they're toys become useless lumps of plastic and glass.

Bugging

One more thing I want to discuss before I step off the soapbox. Two terms you may have heard of: "Bugging Out" and "Bugging In." These are basic concepts, but what do they mean?

Bugging Out

If you live in New York City, Boston, Los Angeles, San Francisco, Chicago, or any other major city, this chapter is for you. If ever a true "Hits the Fan" bad event occurs, what will they do with all the people packed into our major cities?

If there's no power and it looks like it'll stay that way for the foreseeable future, if business as usual (food deliveries, etc.) is not going to return for a while, "Something must be done!" Think about it. New York City with no power. The authorities know that this isn't merely a reset event, where the power will be slowly restored in a matter of hours as is usually the case. This event is caused by or accompanied by some major damage to critical equipment. They know the power isn't going to be restored within a matter of hours, probably not for many days, at least. Then the power grid authorities have bad news – they have no idea how long it is going to take to restore power, there is damage to some major transformers. It could be weeks, it could be months before full power is back! What will they do?

You can wait around the several hours it will take for them to review, discuss, and argue about the finely crafted emergency plan that they've paid a lot of money for, but you will also become more and more at their mercy. If the authorities know the power is not coming back on, will they tell you, and how long will it be before they do? You'll have to play it by ear. If it isn't coming back, they'll call for calm, they'll call for patience. Will they do the absolutely stupidest thing possible, and actually try to prevent people from leaving? That call can be put into action in no time at all. The first few vehicles stopped at all major crossings out will effectively become a roadblock that will become gridlock of historical proportions! I doubt if that'll happen for a power/utility outage. Of course, if the event is a major outbreak of a contagious illness, that might be the smartest call to make.

Oaky, so let's say that the power is out, and it's going to stay off for a long while. What do you think they'll do? I can only guess that eventually you will either be bussed off to FEMA camps (which is ridiculous, there's no place or places available to accommodate so many people, and just how many bus trips will that take, anyway - a few hundred thousand?), or emergency rations will be distributed (as best they can, as they show up) at feeding stations (think of the worst post-apocalyptic movies you've ever seen), or you'll be simply written off. Well, they certainly can't just write-off a city. They will do "Something", that's their job. Whether that "Something" is better than nothing will be debatable, at least in your situation if you are part of the tiny minority of prepared people who, if left alone, could weather the storm for months with little problem.

Let me be fair. Do I think the emergency preparedness of NYC is better than New Orleans pre-Katrina? Yes, light-years better. Do I think any NYC disaster plan is going to survive being put into effect on over 8 million people? Maybe, if given enough time, and there is enough patience amongst the populace. Would I want to wait around to find out just how well the disaster plan worked out, from the inside? HECK NO!

If public hygiene (water, sewers) is off-line or will be shortly, they just can't let people stay there packed together to riot, spread disease, make campfires in the streets, sing "Kumbaya my lord", or whatever it is that 8 million people stuck with no utilities or services and a dwindling food supply will do. Time is not on anyone's side in a case like that. They could just let everyone fend for themselves, but that's hardly likely. What will they do? I know what you should do – "Get Out of Dodge" in a timely and deliberate manner.

Hopefully you'll at least have a pre-selected destination, even better if it was a pre-stocked destination, outside the city, and a plan for getting there as soon as you determine that this might be the Real McCoy. When in doubt, hit the road. I'm not saying if the power goes out, you should immediately grab your bug-out bags and head for the hills. I'm saying to pack the bags if you haven't already done so, get yourselves ready, keep a keen ear to the (battery powered or crank-up) radio, and try your best to determine whether this event will be over tomorrow, or it'll be days or weeks.

Of course, the odds are that not all members of the family will be home at the time this event starts. Parents could be at work, kids at school. No need to freak out. There will be plenty of time for everyone to get home. People aren't going to start rioting in the streets, raping and murdering because of a blackout. Well, probably not. Mostly it's the same situation as I'll discuss in the Security and Defense section – no one will know if this is temporary, long-term, or even permanent situation. The Normalcy Bias will be on your side. Almost everyone will assume that the power will be back "shortly", so they're not going to immediately go berserk. The reality of the situation will take a while to set in.

I was a child of around 10 years old in NYC during the Great Blackout of 1965. I remember it to this day as a kind of big block party with candles and flashlights. It was over in a day.

There wasn't any rioting or looting. There were stories of daring rescues of people from stuck elevators, but that and some extra traffic accidents (no red lights, no green lights) was pretty much the big excitement. Of course, that was 1965 and people for the most part were better behaved then than now. (There was another blackout in 1977, and by then, there was some rioting and looting. Now, it could even be worse.) The power was back on the next day as expected. What if it wasn't?

There were plenty of battery powered and car radios, I assume all the adults knew what was going on, and they weren't freaking out, so as a kid, I thought it was fun. Let's say the next day went by, and there was still no power. The assumption would have been that the power would certainly be back on the day after that. I have no idea how long this would have gone on before some tipping point occurred, and people started getting worried, and took to their cars, or went to the trains, and tried to get out of the city to get to some friend or relative elsewhere.

All you need to do is to determine that it's time to bug out before millions of others take to the roads. When they do, it's going to take a very long time to get out. Once the radio announcers say that the city should be evacuated, it'll be too late. It's taken me a couple of hours to get through NYC on the interstate when nothing at all is wrong. In an evacuation situation, it could take, well, forever? As traffic jams keep people idling in park, some cars will run out of gas, insuring the road will be impassable. Keep in mind, all the boroughs of NYC are islands except the Bronx. Islands have limited ways on and off. Once these bottlenecks get blocked, well, there will be no better alternate routes.

Bugging out is leaving your primary home to go to some other place. It should be to a much safer place than wherever you're leaving from. If it isn't, maybe you should consider bugging-in? Experts don't recommend hiding in the woods, unless you have some Boy Scouts with you to help you survive. Camping out during nice spring/summer weekends is a far cry from being outdoors all winter. When the nuts and berries are all gone, all your stuff is buried in the snow, and the stream/lake is covered in ice (and you're sick of surviving on fish anyway) you may rethink your priorities. Wandering in the wilderness may be better than being stuck in a dead city, but not by much. If you live in the south or west where it winter isn't usually as bad, you may have a better chance than people in the northeast, but just because you live in Charlotte, NC doesn't mean you're a mountain man and can survive in the wilderness!

Living as a hunter/gatherer takes hard work, and an enormous amount of knowledge, the kind of knowledge you can go through high school, college, and graduate school and never get a bit of. Can it be done? Sure. Can you do it? Can you start the learning process through trial and error, when you find yourself out in a forest? Best of luck, and oh, here's another tidbit for you, a little food for thought - there may be no more "hunting seasons", or game tags, or whatever has kept things at least mostly civilized when it comes to hunting in this country. The forests anywhere near a population center are going to be filled with amateur hunters who will be as hungry as you will be. They'll probably be blasting away at anything that moves. Then, possibly, there are people who already live in those woods, who will know the land intimately, will be very good with a rifle, and will not take kindly to a bunch of desperate strangers showing up and cleaning out all their game. If I was one of those people, I'd be picking off every stranger I found. I'll be staying well away from the forest.

Again, if you do decide to Bug Out, you'd better have a destination in mind, and hope that you get going early enough to make it there. You'll need "bug out bags" for each member of the family, with enough supplies (minimally, a few days of food and water, medical and hygiene supplies, and some changes of clothes) to see you through your journey, and a well thought out (and hopefully rehearsed) travel plan.

It may end up being a much longer journey than you'd imagine. Ever see the scenes of the interstate highways on the news, when they are evacuating Miami, or New Orleans, any area where a hurricane is heading (or even been in one of those 50 mile long traffic jams?) Lots of things can happen to you on that particular journey, but getting a speeding ticket probably won't be on that list. Don't wait like the sheep for the news stations to finally tell you to evacuate. Once that happens, it'll be a stampede! Beat the crowd and increase your chances. Plan ahead; know your routes – primary and some backup plans.

Maybe even have a couple of 5 gallon gas cans stored (in a VERY safe manner) with gas stabilizer. If you have a gas lawnmower, you already keep some gas available. At least have some empty gasoline containers handy – they'll be easier to fill than to find if the time comes. If you'd like to hear about a disastrous attempt at evacuating Houston TX for an oncoming Hurricane, I suggest you find Mainprepper on YouTube, he has a great eyewitness account (he also has a wealth of other reputable prepping information). The biggest problem was actually because as the roads get farther from the city, they reduce the number of lanes, slowing down the traffic. Also, because the authorities set both sides of the highways as evacuation routes, no traffic at all could go back towards the city, including gasoline tankers to replenish the gas stations along the route. The problem with that was because of the tens of miles of blocked traffic, people were running out of gas, but there was no longer any gas available along the evacuation routes.

Because vehicles were running out of gas, they compounded the road blockages. People actually began leaving their cars on the highway, and foraging through the adjacent neighborhoods, looking for gasoline and water.

If the "event" happens to be the admittedly super rare possibility that some enemy of the US is able to detonate an EMP blast, either high enough or close enough to your area, it's possible that everyone in the affected area will not be able to start their cars anyway. Most cars are electronic fuel injection these days. If the electronics get fried, your car is going nowhere.

Hopefully you have close friends or relatives living in a, let's say "less congested" area where you can go to wait out whatever happens. When I say "close", I do mean "close!" in both senses of the word. Going from New York City to Idaho, depending on the event, could make for quite an adventure movie someday. As to the other "close", it's going to be far more than a weekend visit, we're talking weeks or even months or longer. It would be a good idea to arrange this well in advance, perhaps even going as far as pre-positioning supplies there. Just showing up at someone's door announcing "Hi! We're here for the duration!" can be regarded as anything from a social faux-pas to an invitation to be murdered in your sleep and buried in the backyard.

I've read that bugging-out to an empty vacation home could be problematic. You'd need to get there early, and the place needs to be secure. Unless you'll be bringing all your supplies with you, you may find it looted by the time you get there, unless you have a very secure means of stashing your supplies. You may even find that others migrating from a population center found your empty place before you get there and already moved in, thinking you're stuck wherever you are, or just won't make it at all. They may be there, and won't want to leave. What are you going to do? Especially if it's a "secret" location.

Just "heading north" or south, or east or west probably won't cut it. North America may have once hosted nomadic tribes, but they were just small populations following the food supply. It was probably as dangerous then as it would be now. You may end up migrating straight into a migration away from some other population center. If you're part of a migration away from a population center, you may find the rest stops are out of gas, the restaurants are out of food, and the local populations along the way aren't going to be too hospitable to strangers. You may also be sharing your migration with folks who aren't as nice as you are. If it gets so bad that it's "every man for himself," it will be very bad indeed.

If you live in a major city, you should definitely learn all you can about Bugging Out – what to take, and how to do it. There are even live classes in Urban Bug-Out! I wouldn't want to be in a city if the food trucks, for whatever reason, stop running for a week or more. That's about how long it will take for all the food on all the store shelves to empty. After that, it might get ugly. Hungry people aren't going to be polite people.

It is possible for city dwellers to bug in, at least for the short term, as long as you keep a low profile and strangers won't know you've got supplies (or if you're even there.) Unfortunately, if the water goes off and you didn't store any, you're screwed. Foraging for water or anything else in a major city during the early part of an event isn't going to be very safe. If the power goes off, well, that's most likely the first thing that happened. Hope you've got a strong door, plus guns and ammo, because eventually you might have "trick or treaters" who aren't little kids with funny costumes. Calling 911 may be an exercise in futility. If you can hold out until the military takes control (which may ultimately be what happens), you'll probably survive. Or wait until things quiet down and sneak away if you can.

Bugging In

I live far from the coast, and my area doesn't flood (I'm only ¼ mile from the CT river (where I'll probably get my water, unless I can someday afford to install a well.) The river might go up 20 feet in a flood, the record is 37 feet, but I'm at least 75 feet, probably closer to 100 feet higher than the river, so I won't get flooded out. Although there have been some minor brush files within several miles of me, there's almost no chance of a forest fire. Although there has been a tornado in my lifetime (up in Springfield, MA), and I think I might have felt an earthquake once, other than blizzards (which I can and have gotten through before with no problem,) there's not much I can think of that will force me to leave due to a natural occurrence.

It's a small town, kind of between two small cities, but it's very suburban and I'm hoping it will be quite a hike for any gangs of urban looters to get to. Not to mention, I can't afford a hideaway out in the woods somewhere, nor do I look forward to living as a hermit. It's unfortunate, but I don't have a bunch of old buddies from when I wasn't in the Special Forces to share my hideaway with. If you're that lucky, you should be thinking along these lines. I can't think of anything safer that having a well-supplied little secret village somewhere to live in, with a dozen or more former Special Forces operators and their families.

Sure, my house can burn down, but anyone's house can burn down anytime. If I've got to go, I'll go – most likely to a neighbor's house who has already bugged out, though. Or to a neighbor who will have to depend on my supplies or starve. There are still some small farms in the area, and depending on the situation, they just might need some help if the busses full of illegal aliens stop showing up. I think there's a good chance of long term survival in my immediate area. I'm hoping, anyway.

There's still a chance I may have to evacuate at some point, either temporarily or permanently, so I'll have a bug-out bag available, with handguns and long guns, ammo, food and water, and clothes appropriate to the season, but that will be a last-ditch decision and I can't foresee a long and prosperous future wandering homeless. I'd be leaving a lot of food and supplies behind, and I really, really won't want to do that.

So now that I've had my turn of the soapbox, time to turn to the specifics. My advice is directed mainly for those who are bugging in.

Water

Water comes first because after any medications you need daily it's the one thing you can't survive without for more than a few days. The most quoted figure I've seen is that you'll need a minimum of a gallon a day per person, and that makes sense. That is 28 gallons a week, 120 gallons a month for a family of 4. That's just for consumption (drinking, reconstituting freeze dried and dehydrated food,) never mind washing and bathing and brushing teeth, cleaning clothes, washing dishes, playing on the "slip and slide," watering the plants, and whatever else you use water for.

All these activities can use many gallons a day of additional water. If you get water bills, check out how many gallons you actually use in a month, or a quarter, and do the math. You may find you've been using 10 or 20 gallons a day or more per person. My point is that you will never be able to store enough water to maintain your current lifestyle if the taps ever run dry. Get it through your head right now – if the event is long enough, you're going to have to find a way to get more water and make it safe to drink. Meanwhile, you should at least store as much as you reasonably can, based on your circumstances.

Storage

Store water in new, food grade "blue" plastic containers specifically made for storing water, to keep chemicals from the plastic container leaching in. Water containers are widely available in everything from 50 gallon drums down to the small containers you take on hikes and to the gym. Have a bit of variety – some large containers for storing and some smaller ones for transporting.

You can get cases of bottled water, but for long term quantity storage, barrels work very well, and I saw a video on You Tube showing what happens when you stack too many water bottle cases – the stack partially collapsed, crushing bottles on the bottom of the stack. It was a mess. There are also emergency sealed "juice paks" and even flexible pre-filled water bags available. That's probably the most costly way to do it, and they would work better for your bug-out bag than for home use. For the home, you should use drums. All major preparedness stores will carry water cans and drums of all sizes. I also found a couple of places that specialize only in storage barrels and drums:

BayTec Containers www.bayteccontainers.com

INFO LINE 888.460.drum (3786)   4761 Hwy 146, Suite 200,

Post Office Box 838, Bacliff, TX 77518

If you want to put in a really big water tank, here's a place to check out:

Plastic-Mart www.plastic-mart.com **866-310-2556**

Store your water in a cool, dark place. The microorganisms that live in water also like warmth and light. Starve them of that and the water will stay safer longer. If you're storing chlorinated municipal water in clean containers, it should last at least a couple of years. You can open a container every year just to check. If there were no microorganisms in the water to begin with, there's no reason it shouldn't be good indefinitely. If you're storing non-chlorinated water, you can add some chlorine bleach (a quarter teaspoon per gallon) or some chlorine dioxide (per package directions) to prevent spoilage.

Drinking nothing but plain water can get pretty boring, so make sure you include lots of "water additives." I stock up on Crystal Lite whenever it's on sale, because I don't enjoy drinking plain water, and I love Crystal Lite Raspberry Lemonade. I've got a big Tupperware container that probably has a year's supply of pouches in it (take the pouches out of the boxes or you're wasting an awful lot of space.)

Of course, the Crystal Lite is just for flavor. A much better choice would be Tang, and that's on my shopping list, too. It's not just orange anymore, and it is a great source of Vitamin C and is also fortified with several other vitamins. As it's a dry powder, unopened containers should last for many years in storage. That's on my shopping list.

There are lots of #10 cans of all sorts of drink mixes on the market, and most giant packs of survival food will contain a number of cans of drink mixes. Some are nothing but sugar and flavoring, just empty calories to boost the daily calorie value of the package while keeping the price down and adding nothing nutritionally. Other mixes are fortified with vitamins, making them more worthwhile. I've seen some mixes that look downright yummy, like chocolate milk, and assorted fruit flavored smoothie mixes. I know we're not in the food section yet, but when I say #10 cans, I mean the specially packed, very-long shelf-life stuff that the survival food manufacturers use. They hold around a gallon of contents. You're not going to find a #10 can of 30 year shelf-life Nestle's Quick on a store shelf, but that doesn't mean you can't properly store any dry powder for many years if it can be kept airtight, cool, and dry, and there are some oxygen scavenger pouches in there.

I've also put away some (well, a lot) of those vacuum bricks of ground coffee, and also a large metal French Press (if you have a glass one, and you break it, you are going to cry) so I can prepare coffee by just pouring in hot water. I've also started stocking up on freeze-dried coffee crystals as I see them on sale. If the jars aren't glass, I'll be transferring the contents to Ball Jars with an oxygen scavenger packet, because most plastic jars aren't really useful for extreme long-term storage. Oxygen can still get through the plastic over time. As with a lot of things, you can't have enough coffee. If you're into it, you should have tea, too. Your favorite varieties can bring much comfort. You can pack teabags into Ball Jars, with an oxygen scavenger, too.

As I've said, storing municipal, treated water should be perfectly safe for at least a couple of years or much longer (potentially indefinitely, but you should check it every year or two as long as you can,) as long as the container and the water was clean to start with.

There is a "drinking water safe" garden hose available on the market, because supposedly the water in normal garden hoses can be infected with bacteria from the hose (which is basically a moist, dark place that sits around outside most, if not all of the year, so that kind of makes sense.) That's up to you, but I fill/refill my little water barrels with chlorinated municipal water in the summer, and I use a regular icky black garden hose, but that's after I've been using the hose a lot. In the summer, it bakes in the sun every day, and I do all my garden watering and basically run the water through the hose for quite a while before I use it to fill the barrels. My water comes out of the tap still smelling a little like chlorine, so I feel safe enough. There are ways to make sure any water is safe to drink (purification,) I'll get to that later.

One gallon of water weighs 8.35 pounds.

30 gallon water barrels (around $70) are just the thing, makes your reserve easy to figure (one a week for a family of 4, or a month for one person) and that's about the largest quantity that is conceivably portable, or at least moveable (250 lbs. filled.) A cheap dolly is worth the investment! The smallest, the 15 gallon barrels (around $50) are much more portable (125 lbs.) A 50 gallon barrel is not very user friendly – it's not going anywhere when filled. If you do use them

make sure it's over a concrete slab in the garage or basement, the weight may test the strength of your floor (417 lbs.)

Make sure, if you buy barrels, you get the whole kit – bung wrench, siphon hose, any adapter needed for the hose. You aren't going to lift and pour from a container that weighs over 100 lbs.! You'll need a way to get the water from the drum into a smaller container. These kits should be available from whoever you buy your drums from.

Significantly smaller containers will be required anyway because you will have to eventually transport water from a river, stream, pond or lake. Even a 5 gallon jug is over 40 lbs.! I've got a couple of 7 gallon jugs with handles for the purpose – it may be almost 60 lbs., but I expect to use a hand truck or garden wagon. Maybe one gallon jugs (milk jug sized) might work for you depending on how much you need, how far the water source is, how many trips you expect to make. Don't use the actual jugs that milk comes in, though, I believe they use biodegradable plastic for them these days, so they may eventually start disintegrating. Don't use glass, either – aside from the extra weight, they're just too easily broken.

I would imagine everyone by now has heard that you can get some emergency water by draining your hot water heater, even draining what remains in your pipes. That'll give you a few days' worth. You can collect rainwater in pre-made systems that people use to collect water for watering their lawns, but if the time ever comes, if your house has rain gutters you can cut them and direct the rain water into containers.

Collected rainwater, river, stream, lake, even reservoir water and melted snow - any water not from your potable well or municipal system (if those sources are even safe) MUST be considered as unsafe for consumption. I don't know how many of you live by a crystal clear Rocky Mountain stream, but even that can contain harmful microorganisms. If it's outdoors, it's probably been contaminated by wildlife. Microorganisms that don't bother them could kill you. Even "distilled" water from solar stills, unless it went through the boiling method, still needs to be treated.

There's water you want, and water you don't want – if you have a sump pump (as I do) in the basement, and there's no electricity, then you won't want to store anything below the flood-line in the basement. I already know that my flood line is around 8-10". I found that out the hard way, before I got a sump pump. Now I keep everything on those plastic shelving units, the first shelf is over a foot above the ground, and even then, nothing that water can ruin goes on that bottom shelf. You can get metal shelving units if you'd like to pay more and don't mind them rusting, although I think having the metal units is the only way your shelving units can have wheels, which might be of benefit to you depending on how much room you've got.

I'm fortunate in that I'll know if my sump pump is going to be running based of the snowpack and/or the rainfall amount. I'll have time to move everything from the basement upstairs. If you have a basement and it can flood, you'll have to take that into consideration. If the power is going to be out for an appreciable amount of time, I'll have to move everything from my basement upstairs. There may not be room now, but I'll make room if the time ever comes. The only silver lining is that the water that seeps into the basement (during the right season) can be made into potable water, which will save me some trips to the river!

Before I forget to tell you, you shouldn't store plastic water barrels directly on concrete. Don't put metals directly on it either. Actually, don't store anything directly on concrete just to be safe. At the very least, put a few sheets of cardboard (flattened shipping boxes would do the trick,) a folded up plastic or fabric tarp, or a piece of plywood down first. Concrete isn't an inert stone, it still is somewhat porous and even slightly chemically active (somewhat caustic from what I recall reading) and I've read a lot of warnings about not putting this or that directly on the concrete floor. It will definitely cause metals to rust faster, and there could possibly be some chemical leaching into some containers. It's best to just not store anything directly on concrete without some other, safer material in between.

Fortunately, water may be one of the last things to become unavailable; maybe a while after the power goes out. Unless it's an EMP attack, in which case everything electrical will burn out, and that includes emergency generators. Many municipal water systems can operate for some time on backup diesel power. Some systems have water towers. You've probably seen them; driving down the highway, they're big tanks sitting up on towers - they usually have the town's name on it, and maybe a bunch of graffiti, too. They insure that there will be water pressure due to gravity. Water has to be pumped up into them, though. At least the towers will be good until drained (which shouldn't take long, as your idiot neighbors continue to take long showers, and possibly water their lawns with what may have become a precious commodity that should be reserved for consumption only.

Well Water

If you have your own potable water well, you're very lucky. You'll have minimal need for storage (as long as the underground water source lasts). If you know it's good potable water there will no purification requirement (and even if it's not potable you probably know why, and can treat it for just the specific impurities you know it has), and certainly there will be no hauling water from afar.

If all you have is an electric well pump, you'll need to have electricity for the pump to work. If you do have a water well, an investment in a manual mechanical pump is essential – you have an almost permanent source of water that depends on the most vulnerable component of our modern world. Even if you have a generator, what happens if it breaks, or you run out of fuel? Get a simple hand pump, just like they used in the olden days, and that we've all seen in the TV & movie westerns. Put your bucket under the spigot, and pump, pump, pump the handle, and out comes water! You don't even need to use a bucket – with the right setup you can even pump it straight into your home plumbing. You can be taking a shower in your own bathroom, while I'm standing under a tree with a camping shower (as long as someone is manning the pump for you).

Electric and manual well pumps can coexist in the same well at the same time. As long as the width of the well is larger than the width of the two pipes. Most wells will be 5 or 6 inches, and most of the pipe will be not more than one to two inches thick.

I had a water well in a previous home, and had no idea they still had manual pumps, costing from as little as $100 to over $1,000 depending on the well depth and the type and quality of the components you buy. The manual pump can be in your well at the same time as, and will not interfere with your electric pump. The bottom of the device sits submerged, but above the level of your electric well pump (which is usually at the bottom of the well). If your power goes out (or even if the pump dies), you need only pump the water you need manually. It can be set up so that you can even pump the water into your regular home plumbing, so the water will come out through the faucets in your home – as long as someone is manning the pump. Yes, it will be cold water, but that's better than nothing.

Before you even start shopping for a manual pump system, you'll need to know the diameter of your well (probably 5 or 6 inches, but measure to be sure). You also need to know the depth of the well and the water level inside the well.

Get a spool of cord or string that is longer than your well is deep. How long is that? How should I know? Do you have a 90 foot well, or a 300 foot well? Could be less, could be more. If you've got no idea, maybe your well service company knows. Or just get a 500 foot roll, which should be long enough. Tie a (clean! It's going into your water) heavy washer or fishing weight to the end of the line, and start letting it unroll into your well. When it stops pulling, that's most likely the bottom of the well (or maybe it's the top of your well pump, but that's close enough. Mark the line or knot it, you'll be measuring it later. From this point to the weighted end is the overall well depth. As you pull the line up, stop when you get to the wet part and mark or knot it again – that's the top of your water level. After you get the string all the way out of the well, use a yardstick or any other method to take the following measurements. From the bottom (weighted end) to where it goes from wet to dry, this could be just a few feet to tens of feet – that's your water level, how high the water is from the bottom of the well. Then from that point to the other point that you marked, added to the water level, is overall the depth of your well.

These measurements are really important, because you're going to have to know how much piping you'll have to buy. The bottom of the pump mechanism has to be in the water, and the top has to be at the surface. It would be a waste of money to buy 300 feet of pipe to find out you've got an 80 foot well, but you definitely don't want to buy 150 feet of pipe to find out you've got a 200 foot well! Especially if you aren't installing it immediately! I know if I had a well, I wouldn't wait to assemble and test my manual pump, I'd want it in there and working. If you buy a manual pump setup to store in the garage till it's needed, if I were you, I would at least open the box to make sure nothing was forgotten, and nothing looks broken. If you have to break out the manual pump because of a major event, it's probably not a good time to contact the manufacturer because there's a part missing! It's probably also a bad time to go shopping for PVC glue. Not to mention, you're going to need time and some help on this project. You'll most likely be using PVC piping, and it will come in sections no longer than 8-12 feet, so you'll be gluing sections together at the surface. Then, when your glue joints have set, you'll need a few more hands to help you fish this thing down your well. PCV is flexible, but it's not garden hose!

There's one more thing I want to tell to you based on what I've learned about this whole process. The bottom of the pump needs to be within the water level down at the bottom of the well. It should also not sit all the way on the bottom. One system suggested that the bottom of the pipe be around the middle of the water level, but I'd go lower than that, in case the water table underground was higher when you measured it than when you'll actually need the water. There could be five or ten feet of water down there. To keep the bottom of the pipe above the bottom of the well, the total pipe length should be a shorter than the top of the well. Meaning that if you screw up as you fish the pipe down the well, and it slips out of your hand and falls to the bottom, you're going to have a heck of a time trying to reach into the well pipe to grab that pipe to pull it back out.

Just in case you're missing some common sense, please make sure the pipe is longer than the well is deep, and trim the excess pipe off after you have set it into the well. The kit should have a device that will hold the pipe at the top of the well, preventing it from slipping down. While you're installing this device, you really should have something tied to the top of the pipe so you can pull it out if you screw up and it slips. If you can afford to, you can pay a local well service do the installation for you.

Here's a selection of manual well pump manufacturers I've found. I know nothing about any of them as unfortunately I don't have a well, so I have no use for one (but I surely wish I did):

Bison Pumps www.bisonpumps.com

1-800-339-2601 PO Box 977, Houlton, Maine 04370

Simple Pump www.simplepump.com

1-877-492-8711, 775-265-4908 1140 Amarillo Drive, Gardnerville, Nevada 89460-7504

Flojack Pump www.flojak.com

1-855-435-6525 408 Ironworks Drive, Mountain View, Arkansas 72560

Oasis Pumps Manufacturing Co. www.oasispumps.com

812-783-2146 3001 Curtis Rd. Mt. Vernon, IN 47620

Make your water safe to drink.

If it isn't properly stored drinking water, you have to do something to make sure there is nothing in the water that will make you sick – or worse.

Your enemies include protozoa, viruses, bacteria, and inorganic pollutants (like pesticides or heavy metals such as lead.) Let's get scary. The biggest microorganisms that you can't even see are protozoa like giardia and cryptosporidium (and lots more.) Smaller, there's E. Coli (the stuff that's been killing and making people sick in big numbers every year, it usually comes from human or animal poop), cholera, salmonella, and again, lots more. Smaller still, there are viruses like hepatitis, rotavirus, poliovirus, and yes, again, many more. Smallest are just molecules of pollutants like heavy metals and metal salts. Ever hear of lead? It's a metal, it's pretty heavy, and it's a relatively common water pollutant. It can also damage the brain and nervous system, especially of small children. Some of these are very common, others are pretty rare. Don't take chances. You might have swallowed a mouthful of lake or river water at some time in your life. If you're reading this now, it didn't kill you. Maybe it didn't make you sick. Want to take that chance with every swallow? Put your loved ones through the same risk? Hopefully not. I suggest using at least one, if not two out of the three purification methods if you can (filtration and either heat or chemical,) which are:

Heat purification:

> **Pasteurization** (heating to over 150 degrees, uses less fuel than boiling, and is pretty effective),

> **Boiling** (that's 212 degrees, will kill just about all targeted microorganisms),

> **Distilling** (heating up to and including boiling, and then capturing and condensing the vapor back to a liquid. As effective as it is, it's a very slow and very limited quantity method, using a lot of fuel). You can include solar stills in distillation, but the process is primarily used for converting

salt water to fresh, it's not a good way to purify potentially contaminated water.

Chemical purification:

Iodine treatment (not the most effective, but better than nothing, but not for long-term use and certainly not for pregnant women and people with thyroid conditions),

Chlorine bleach (kills most everything except cryptosporidium, including you if you don't do it right, it's the most common and least expensive chemical treatment),

Chlorine dioxide (also kills most everything, but safer to use than bleach, though much more expensive than bleach),

There's even a use for Silver and Ultraviolet light in water purification, but those methods probably aren't going to be available to you for purifying large quantities of water so they're not worth discussing in detail. Some more exotic filter systems use silver in them, but silver alone? I don't know about that. There's also peroxide, but that too, isn't recommended unless it's a last resort.

Filtration:

Several varieties are available, but the Brita and Pure Pitchers are not acceptable for purification. They're for making potable tap water taste better, not much more. If that's all you have, you won't be able to make your water safe. Real water filtration, removing harmful micro-organisms, heavy metals, and assorted other pollutants takes special filters, made for the purpose.

Reverse osmosis:

Usually used to make fresh water from salt water, it depends of having water forced through a membrane under pressure. This method is usually what could be considered an industrial process, but there actually are personal sized systems available.

No matter what your water source (but use the best source available – moving, cold water is better than stagnant warm water,) you should at least filter it enough to make it clear before you try to make it safe to drink. Rags, old clothes, nylon stockings stuffed with cloth, anything like that would be a great first filtration step, just to make it clear. You can even make your own sand filter as a pre-stage. Sand is good for large quantities and does a respectable job. There are directions for making sand filters all over the internet. If you're going to go to the trouble, you may as well make sure you have a layer of charcoal in addition to sand.

Don't start the purification process with muddy or other cloudy crappy stuff in the water, use a pre-filter.

Anything that will take out all the "big pieces" is fine, as you aren't going to drink the stuff anyway. Water that looks clean to the naked eye can kill you – slowly and painfully. Especially since, if the situation is such that you have to make your own water, the odds of ending up in the emergency room hooked up to intravenous drips of antibiotics will probably not be very high, unless you've got that stashed away in your basement. The odds of ending up writhing around in pain, sweating profusely and spewing from both ends are a much better bet.

Have I scared you yet? Good! If I've got you scared enough, you might not sicken yourself and everyone in your group. Like I said, you might have swallowed a mouthful of river or lake water once in a while and got lucky, but don't take any chances. In 1993, Milwaukee, Wisconsin residents got a bad batch of lake water in their municipal water system and it killed over 100 people and made an additional 400,000 people sick to varying degrees. Thousands and thousands of people get sick each year from presumably safe sources of drinking water. Do you want to take your chances with presumably (let's say certainly) unsafe water? If you live downstream from a major city, and there's a significant breakdown of the social order, you may end up with some pretty crummy water, indeed. Want to drink water that has human bodies and raw sewage floating around in it? Even that can be made drinkable, if you're careful to do it right. You might have no choice anyway – I won't. Hey, residents of Springfield, Massachusetts – let's take it easy on the filth you dump in the river, okay?

Filtration

Get the best device or system can afford, and as many replacement filters too. The Brita or Pure filter pitcher in your refrigerator is good for making tap water taste better and very little else. Other filters on the market, like the Zero Water filter, will do a better job (at a much higher price), but only for small quantities. There are other, purpose built filters made for campers and backpackers that will pretty much make any clear water potable. Remember what I said earlier, if the water you start with isn't clear and clean-looking, you can use almost anything as a pre-filter so you don't clog up your real filters prematurely. The best filters do not even need any chemical or heat treatment to make the water safe.

There are several manufacturers of water filter systems that you can use to purify large amounts of water. Some use hand cranked pumps (one tube in the supply of "bad water", another tube in the receptacle for your good water, and the cranking action will pump the water through the filter); some use gravity to force the water through the filtering agent (fill the top receptacle with bad water and gravity will force the water through the filter to the collection receptacle.)

Even within the same brand, the filters themselves have various levels of effectiveness and price points. You should expect to spend anywhere from around $50 for a decent camping filter good for just a few hundred gallons to maybe a few hundred dollars for a high-throughput system and the minimum amount of disposable filter cartridges you need. (My system uses either 2 or 4 "candles"). You can buy more filters later as you add to your supplies over time.

Remember, there is a chance you may have to purify several thousand gallons of water over time. The minimum is for consumption, a gallon a day per person. Then, there is tooth brushing (yeah, definitely must use potable water for that); bathing (I'd want at least chlorinated water for that, I had a professor once who was blind in one eye and said it was because he picked up an amoeba in lake when he was young); clothes washing (didn't they used to pound clothes on rocks at the riverbank to clean them? I think they still do, somewhere in the world. That water doesn't need to be potable, but it still makes me itch thinking about it) and anything else you can think of. It's up to you to determine what quality of water you'll need for any purpose (except if you drink it, put it in your mouth, eyes, clean wounds, rinse eating utensils, it better be your best potable water, or you're an idiot!)

You will want to make sure the filters have an activated charcoal stage that will handle inorganic stuff like lead and heavy metals. It should also be antibacterial, so the filter itself doesn't start sprouting goo.

If fuel won't be in great supply or you feel that boiling all your water will be a pain in the butt, then you might want to use high quality filters as well as chlorine bleach or chlorine dioxide to kill off the little buggers. If you're only going to filter, save up, and get the very best you can afford.

If you think your future water supply may have heavy metals (and nothing's stopping you from getting a sample and having it tested right now,) you'll want to make sure you get a filter that will handle it.

You are likely going to be boiling a batch of water a couple times a day just for making coffee/tea and reconstituting food or boiling rice/beans. I hope I don't need to point out that you shouldn't be re-boiling water that you've already boiled. Keep a container of filtered or chemically treated water for that purpose.

If you boil water, make sure you let it get to room temperature before you filter it, if that's the way you want to roll. I don't know if there's a warning on ceramic filters, but common sense tells me that pouring boiling water on a ceramic anything may lead to cracking. A cracked filter is a worthless rock.

Again, filter systems range from tens of dollars to hundreds of dollars, and only you can decide what your budget will permit. You can get a good system and just a couple of filters to start with, and stock up on more filter cartridges over time. Even if you have your own well, and it's always tested out good, has it ever gone dry? Gotten polluted from groundwater? Water is so critical for survival it may be wise to have a backup for your backup.

Spend some time on the following websites (there are probably more manufacturers out there, but these are enough to get you started, there isn't going to be much more variety in the technology.)

See what is available, pick what you're comfortable with, and then go shopping for the best price. I personally have a Berkey system with Black Berkey filters, as well as three Katadyn filters.

There are Doulton Filter systems that are used by international relief agencies in the third world; they know how to protect you from nasty creepy stuff (although Berkey has

taken the idea a step further with their improvements on the filter cartridges.) This type of system has a raw water basin above, the water flows through the filters into a clean water tank below

www.doulton.com

800-696-1435

Katadyn is pretty much the king of backpacking, hiking, and camping water filtration, and are widely sold. They are Swiss made, and outdoorspeople the world over swear by them. Unlike the other filter systems, you can actually carry these around, potentially in a big pocket, and drink out of any water source you run across. I have three of them: www.katadyn.com

Berkey filters systems are similar to the Doulton Systems (and also use Doulton filter modules for some of their systems.) There are different varieties of Berkey filters; they can be used just for microorganisms, and also for heavy metals and other pollutants. These guys seem more directed at the Preparedness community. These are systems for filtering larger quantities of water. I have one of these, with their Black Candle (filter), which is probably the best filter made. It's actually allowed to be called a purifier instead of a filter it's so good! At around $50

each, they'd better be the best. Of course, it's rated for I think 3,000 gallons, so it's really one of the least expensive filters per gallon. It would serve you well to read up about the ceramic candle type of water purification systems: www.bigberkeywaterfilters.com www.berkeywaterfilters.com

I've got the clear plastic model. The stainless models will look great in a kitchen with all stainless appliances, but this baby is probably the most key component of all my survival gear, and I wanted it to be light enough to carry around if needed. I don't know what the stainless ones weigh, but the plastic one is extremely light.

There are DIY filter kits available, too. I'd prefer a commercially made system, but there is no shortage of alternatives available. None of which are going to do the whole job, but as pre-filters, they will extend the life of the "real" filters by getting rid of a lot of the solids. If you can integrate the "real" Doulton or Berkey filter candles into a DIY system, then you won't need anything else:

www.reuk.co.uk/Sand-Filters-for-Greywater.htm

www.tacticalintelligence.net/blog/how-to-make-a-homemade-water-filter.htm

Heat Treatment

Heat treatment in an environment without electricity means fire or sunlight. Fire needs fuel, which will never be in unlimited supply. Fire, especially if there is smoke, can also advertise your presence far and wide, which is not a good idea. Even the smell of cooking food can bring all the unprepared neighbors around with hopes of a meal. I'll discuss that in more depth later.

You can boil all your water, which would be ideal, but it uses a lot of fuel, and technically, you can say it wastes fuel, because it doesn't really have to be boiled. It doesn't hurt, boil it for an hour if you have the fuel to waste, but you can actually pasteurize water, which is just bringing it to over 150 degrees. Higher temperatures are better, but they did studies in Africa with the crappy water they find there, and found that even the worst critters die in the 150's. There are links to the utility of water Pasteurization in the second link below:

The wood fueled jet-cooker I bought (www.stovetec.net) also has a Pasteurizer attachment:

http://www.stovetec.net/us/index.php?option=com_content&vie
w=article&id=152&Itemid=695

The Pasteurizer is like a big tea kettle, equipped with a thermometer. The "thermometer" is basically a sealed tube with a plug of wax in it. The wax melts at 150 degrees, and runs down inside the tube to show the water is at the right temperature. You can keep the water cooking till it boils if you are reconstituting a meal or making coffee or tea, but if you just need safe water, you can stop feeding the flame at that point.

I also have a kerosene fueled stove, but although kerosene is pretty safe to store, there's a limit to how much I'll have available, and I'm pretty sure I'll have more water to boil than kerosene to boil it. I'd rather limit my kerosene use to cooking, and indoor heating and lighting.

There are also solar powered "ovens" available, but that's a very slow, if fuel-free method. I'll be doing more research on those myself, as it'll allow you to use any sunny day to save on fuel. You can boil water with them as well as cook food.

If I know the event will be relatively short-lived, then cooking and boiling would be a good use of the limited fuel I'd have available. I should be able to find a good amount of wood, but probably not seasoned, dry wood. Depending on where you live, you might have wood in abundance. Either way, fire needs fuel. Fuel will not necessarily be as available as it is now, and if you decide that you're going to boil all your water, you're going to need a lot of fuel, maybe more fuel than you're going to find available. Keep your limited fuel for cooking and heating, and in my case, boiling water to reconstitute freeze dried food and making rice and beans.

Desalinization

If you live by a body of salt water, and there is no fresh water available within a reasonable distance, and you have no well, you will have to either bug out when your stored water is almost depleted, or make fresh water from salt water. This is difficult, expensive, or both. Some people (like me) would think that if you have an oceanfront view in the first place, it's got to be worth it to invest several thousand dollars to make sure you always have drinking water, at least if you're not planning to bug out.

There are really only two ways to desalinate water. You can use a reverse-osmosis filtration system, or distillation.

For producing very small quantities of fresh water, like half a liter per day, there's a system sold through http://www.homedepot.com called the Seapack Emergency Desalinization Filter (also available with different packaging at some emergency suppliers, but for more money). At Home Depot, for $45 (todays price) each kit will make ½ liter (17 oz.) of fresh potable water a DAY for up to 8 days.

Get a bunch if you've got a big family. It will be barely enough to keep you from dying of thirst, at least for a few extra days. This will definitely not keep you in sufficient water.

Fortunately for you, Katadyne has a couple of hand pump systems that produce enough pressure to use an osmosis filter. These systems actually look promising, in that they will make enough fresh water each day to keep a whole family going indefinitely, as long as you have enough spare parts (and I'd get spares of the whole thing if I were you. If you break it, you're bugging out!)

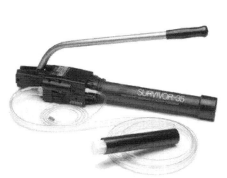

This one, for around $2,000 will do about 1.2 gallons an hour. A few hours of pumping every day, and this baby will let you hold out indefinitely. Make sure you have plenty of spare parts stocked. They don't mention on their website how much water you can make before you have to do maintenance or change out parts, but considering the spare parts list, there's going to be a fair amount of that to do. These are EMERGENCY systems; they're not made to work every day for months at a time. If you only get one, and it breaks, you are going to cry. Unlike breaking a French Coffee Press, you'll not only cry, you may also die.

There's a smaller one that's only about $800 which makes 30 ounces an hour. They also have models that work on 12 volt dc (car or boat batteries) if you're set up for that. They'll supposedly also work with electricity  generated by solar, too. What the heck, just go to the website and look at everything.

There are bigger (non-industrial) systems I've seen that are marketed to boaters, but whatever you end up with, make sure it is capable of producing at least 1 gallon per day per person, which I think they should all do easily. It should make a lot more than the minimum; you'll need to store up the difference for when you run out of fuel, or have to switch to the manual pumps. There are also commercial scale distillation systems available. One system I've seen requires propane as the fuel, also marketed to the boating community. There are devices that you can buy or build called "solar stills", which uses sunlight to heat the water till it evaporates, and the water is condensed on plastic sheeting and drips into a collector. You may get a few cups a day with one of those. It does not kill microorganisms.

If you live on the coast, you should learn all you can about these systems and determine and purchase what's best for your situation. Except for the manual pumps and the solar still, both methods require a big ratio of fuel to water, or require electricity. This is something you need to figure out before an event. If you wait until your taps run dry, you're going to get very thirsty, and whether on land or at sea, you can't live on seawater much longer than you can on no water.

Chemical Treatment

You can and should filter the water, and you can optionally heat the water. You can also chemically treat the water in several different ways. Chlorine is the most commonly used (and least expensive) water disinfectant, but there's also iodine, and chlorine dioxide. I've seen people talk about using peroxide, but after reading up about it, I rate it unacceptable. It doesn't do a great job, and the biggest pro seems to be that there will be more oxygen in your water. Sorry, but there's no scientific evidence that having more oxygen in your water is any benefit, except for fish. Last I heard, your stomach isn't involved in the breathing process.

Chlorine does a great job, except on one particular critter (it's a protozoa, so it's one of the big ones.)

(Nothing says there will definitely be cryptosporidium in any particular body of water, but it seems that it could be present in any body of water, including swimming pools.)

Excerpted from the Wikipedia article:

"Cryptosporidium oocysts are extremely resistant to chlorine. The use of chlorine
alone should not be expected to inactivate *C. parvum* oocysts in drinking water. *Cryptosporidium* is highly resistant to chlorine disinfection, however with high enough concentrations and contact time, *Cryptosporidium* inactivation will occur with chlorine dioxide and ozone treatment. The required levels of chlorine (very high) generally preclude the use of chlorine disinfection as a reliable method to control *Cryptosporidium* in drinking water... common filtration processes including slow sand filters, diatomaceous earth filter, and membranes will remove 99% of *Cryptosporidium*. Membranes and bag- and cartridge-filter products remove *Cryptosporidium* specifically. For the end consumer of drinking water believed to be contaminated by *Cryptosporidium*, the safest option is to boil all water used for drinking.

Cases of cryptosporidiosis can occur in a city that does not have a contaminated water supply. In a city with clean water, it may be that cases of cryptosporidiosis have different origins. Testing of water, as well as epidemiological study, are necessary to determine the sources of specific infections. Note that *Cryptosporidium* typically does not cause serious illness in healthy people.

Cryptosporidiosis is typically an acute short-term infection but can become severe and non-resolving in children and immuno-compromised individuals. In humans, it remains in the lower intestine and may remain for up to five weeks. The parasite is transmitted by environmentally hardy cysts (oocysts) that, once ingested, excyst in the small intestine and result in an infection of intestinal epithelial tissue.

It may chronically sicken some children, as well as adults who are exposed and immunocompromised. A subset of the immuno-compromised population is people with AIDS. Some sexual behaviours can transmit the parasite directly."

From the FDA website:

"Infectious dose--Less than 10 organisms and, presumably, one organism can initiate an infection. The mechanism of disease is not known; however, the intracellular stages of the parasite can cause severe tissue alteration."

And:

"*Cryptosporidium* sp. could occur, theoretically, on any food touched by a contaminated food handler. Incidence is higher in child day care centers that serve food. Fertilizing salad vegetables with manure is another possible source of human infection. Large outbreaks are associated with contaminated water supplies."

"Intestinal cryptosporidiosis is self-limiting in most healthy individuals, with watery diarrhea lasting 2-4 days. In some outbreaks at day care centers, diarrhea has lasted 1 to 4 weeks. To date, there is no known effective drug for the treatment of cryptosporidiosis. Immunodeficient individuals, especially AIDS patients, may have the disease for life, with the severe watery

diarrhea contributing to death. Invasion of the pulmonary system may also be fatal."

What does this all mean? "Crypto" will rarely kill you, but you may wish you were dead. If it is in your water, and it *could* be in *any* water, chlorine alone won't get rid of it. You also need to filter the water and/or boil the water. Fortunately, the filters I recommend get rid of crypto.

Household Bleach

Surprisingly, the simplest, cheapest, and also most effective method to sterilize water is using plain old household chlorine bleach. My tap water has a residual chlorine smell, so I know they use it for my municipal water. I hope I don't have to remind you that you need to keep track of which containers are for contaminated water and which are for safe water. Putting good water into a container that is has been used for contaminated water without first thoroughly cleaning the container with a strong bleach solution will just contaminate the good water and you'll have to start over again. It might be a good idea to mark your containers with an indelible (magic) marker "clean only" and "dirty only" so no one gets mixed up.

First of all, start with the clearest water possible, run it through a pre-filter (an old sock will do) just to keep as much of the solids out as possible. The more solids, the more it will use up the chlorine, so you'll have to use a lot more bleach if the water is cloudy than if it is clear.

Using "fresh" household liquid bleach, add "about" 16 drops, or ¼ teaspoon of fresh household bleach (use the kind with no perfumes, other cleaners, or any other additive at all) per gallon.

Cap and shake the container. Let it sit for at least half an hour. Uncap, let it air out a bit, and then cautiously sniff. There should be a slight, but distinct aroma of chlorine. If there is no aroma at all, you <u>must</u> repeat the process. If your nose doesn't work normally, you may want to let someone else take care of the "smell" testing for you. If you don't get the chlorine aroma, that means that all the free chlorine was all used up before it could adequately disinfect all the water. On the other hand, if the chlorine smell is so strong it makes your eyes water, it's too much to drink. Letting the water sit in an open container in sunlight will let the chlorine leave the water, and you can speed it along by pouring up and back from one container to another to aerate it, and so as long as no dirt is going to get into the container, let it sit opened for a few hours. Don't go too far overboard on the bleach dosage. You need enough to do the job, but if the concentration gets too high, you can't drink it until the chlorine content goes way down. You should notice a slight smell of chlorine, not none at all, and not enough to be irritating.

Note - bleach loses its potency a lot over time and it only starts at 5% to 6% concentration to start with – year old bleach will need as much as twice the dosage as fresh bleach and it doesn't even matter if it's been in the refrigerator. There's a study (bleach for purifying water is so important worldwide, that a LOT of scientists have been studying bleach) that showed that refrigerated bleach (5% Sodium Hypochlorite solution) lost 47% of its concentration in a year, 53% at room temperature and over 60% stored in direct sunlight.

http://www.gewater.com/handbook/cooling_water_systems/ch_2 7_chlorine.jsp

http://www.clorox.com/blogs/dr-laundry/2011/12/28/shelf-life-odor/

This is fair-used directly from the Chlorox website:

Q: My Clorox® Regular-Bleach has lost its odor, what is the shelf life of bleach?

A: It's important to keep track of how old your bleach is because yes, bleach doesn't last forever! When Clorox® Regular-Bleach is stored between 50°F and 70F° and away from sunlight, it will maintain label strength of the sodium hypochlorite active for up to 6 months (at this point hospitals should replace it). After 6 months it starts breaking down into salt and water, but will still perform well for home consumer cleaning needs for up to a year. Since it's always diluted before use, you can just use a little more. Beyond a year, it should be replaced because the rate of decomposition into salt and water really speeds up, a big part of why it's so environmentally friendly.

The best way to identify the age of a bottle (people don't always remember when they bought it!) is to use the production code stamped on the neck of the bottle, which typically looks like this:

A8116010

5813-CA3

The information on when the bleach was made is in the top line, which would be A8-1-160-10 if you added dashes. You only need the first 6 digits and you read it from left to right as follows:

Plant Number—Last digit of year made—Day of the year made

A8   1   160

The bleach in this example was made in 2011 on June 9th, the 160th day of the year.

Calcium Hypochlorite ("Pool Shock")

Calcium Hypochlorite has some advantages over household bleach. If you can find it, it's not as easy to find in stores as I thought. Most pool treatments seem to include a lot of other ingredients like anti-algae chemicals you don't want to drink, nor treat your water with. It has a much longer shelf-life (I've seen figures quoted from 2 years to 10 years, and I'd guess a lot depends on how well it's packaged;) it's also cheaper, and much more concentrated than plain household bleach. It's also much more dangerous than using household bleach, so unless you can be careful and do things properly, you might want to stick to household bleach even though you need to remember that the older the bleach is, the more you have to use. Using the CH, you're basically making your own batches of fresh bleach each time. You're also handling an extremely toxic, poisonous material that can burn your skin, make you blind, and even kill you. So be extremely careful. If fact, if you chose to use the CH method for purifying your water, you should have a bucket of clean, pure water within reach so you can dunk your head in it or have someone pour it over you if you screw this up. Somewhat like if you set yourself on fire.

You need to start out with pre-filtered water (no "turbidity"), clean and without sediment or stuff floating in it. Let the water stand overnight if you can't filter it, then pour off anything that's floating, and then pour off the clear water – gently – so any settled solids stay at the bottom. Solids in the water reduce the effectiveness of chlorine treatment.

The formula I found is to add a bit less than a teaspoon (not a tablespoon) to a gallon of water. Never add water to the powder, always add the powder to the water. Why? If you begin to add water to the powder, you will immediately create a very concentrated solution that will start throwing off chlorine gas like crazy, just a whiff of it will mess up your lungs permanently, and if it gets in your eyes you'll be blinded. Ever hear of the use of chlorine gas during World War I? Google it sometime. It was called poison gas, and it's a prohibited weapon of mass destruction. If the wind blows the smallest speck of this compound into your eye, kiss your eyesight goodbye. So have your FILLED gallon container of water ready, get your teaspoon with a bit less than a teaspoon of powder in it, and at arms-length, dump it in the water. It would be advisable to use gloves, safety glasses, and some sort of safety mask on while playing with pool shock, but we both know you're going to play he-man and not bother with such pansy precautions. When millions of pool owners all over the country have been dumping packets of this stuff in their pool every summer, why go overboard on precautions? So I'm going to tell you not to do this at all, so don't sue me if you do and something goes wrong.

So if you've managed to prepare this gallon of "mother solution" without fatally injuring yourself, you can now use it as you use household bleach. You can use it for cleaning and sanitizing. You can add a quarter teaspoon per gallon to treat your drinking water, as with household bleach. As with household bleach, time and exposure to sunlight will let the free chlorine leave the solution, but if you treated the water and let it sit for half an hour, you should definitely detect the smell of chlorine or do the treatment again. Maybe if the solution is too weak, you can add a full teaspoon or more per gallon. The point is to add enough so that you can smell the chlorine after it has been sitting for a good half hour.

I've read that there are different types of pool shock, and not being a pool owner myself, I can only go by what I read. You can get the stuff quite widely: Pool supply stores, Home Depot, Wal-Mart, I've even seen it at some "dollar" stores. You want to use the types that are EPA approved for treatment of potable water. There are some kinds that aren't pure calcium hypochlorite, as I said, they have anti-algae chemicals in it too. That's going to take a little research on the web.

Storing CH properly is important. It's very chemically active, and moisture will react with it. It will give off chlorine gas. What remains will be calcium carbonate (Tums anti-acid.) So it's not what remains that's the problem, it's the chlorine it gives off. It's best stored in plastic containers made from the same plastic that the stuff comes in, because the manufacturers don't want their packages to dissolve on the store shelves. Polyethylene containers are best. I've read that squeezable Nalgene brand bottles marked as LDPE, HDPE, or UVPE are good, but Polycarbonate and Lexan (hard plastics) are not suitable. It's best to get a container that your CH will fit into without removing it from its original packaging. If you can't get a suitable container, just leave it be, unopened, and in a cool, dry place. Heat and sunlight does bad things to it, from releasing chlorine gas to combustion (bursting into flames!) Just to be safe, don't store it with foods, or anything else that can be ruined by chlorine gas, because it's always going to give off at least a little bit that may seep through the packaging. If you do manage to find a container for it, don't open the container till you're out in fresh air so any chlorine gas that built up in the container can dissipate when you open it. One website reports that the 1 lb. sacks of HTH Shock-n-Swim will fit into a 1 litre HDPE Nalgene bottle, but the guy had first tried using a glass jar with a rubber gasket on the lid, and it made the lid rust out.

I know that you'll need an advanced degree to be able to calculate the "parts per million (ppm)" of the solutions you'll be making, but here's a list I've found, use the ppm as a relative guide (2 ppm is double 1 ppm, 100 ppm is of course 100 times the concentration of 1 ppm, etc.)

Pure Calcium Hypochlorite is about 70% free chlorine (700,000 parts per million)

Household bleach is about 5% free chlorine (50,000 ppm)

You need between 0.1 to 1% for bleaching laundry (1,000-10,000ppm)

OSHA and the EPA allows restaurants to clean dishes and food preparation surfaces with 200 ppm without having to rinse afterwards.

Wastewater needs 60ppm, clean clear water only needs 1ppm. Lake water and hard water with minimal algae needs 2ppm. So you really don't need to stock up on too much CH, I read that a pound of the stuff could disinfect 100,000 gallons of water.

The amount of chlorine needed varies with what is already in the water. I say again, the bottom line is that you should add enough to be able to smell the free chlorine after the water sits for half an hour. If the smell is very strong, if it is obnoxious, if it makes your eyes water, just let the water sit uncovered, or pour it between containers to aerate it a few times. The free chlorine will leave the water over time.

Iodine

There are water treatment kits available with iodine, usually you add one iodine tablet to the water, and after that has time to do its magic, you add another tablet that causes the iodine to precipitate (come out of solution.) Iodine is harmful to pregnant women, and to people with some illnesses, doesn't work well on all types of critters, and makes the water taste bad (so I hear, I've no intention of trying it, although I do have one of these kits I picked up somewhere.)

Chlorine Dioxide

There's another treatment called chlorine dioxide. It sterilizes like chlorine, but doesn't release the free chlorine that bleach does. Chlorine dioxide is commonly used to treat water and to sterilize commercial kitchens, and it's effective - they even used it to get rid of anthrax. It's nowhere near as inexpensive as bleach, but if you can't stand the smell of bleach, packs of chlorine dioxide tablets are pretty widely available for you to buy, too. The label will tell you how many tablets to use for whatever amount of water you're treating. It's best for the short term, it'll get really expensive to use for a year's supply of water. The average price I've seen is about fifty cents a tablet, and each tablet is good for about a quart. Unless you can find a great way to get this stuff wholesale, think about how $2 a day per person for the minimum amount of water is going to add up over time.

Summary

Pick your poison, add to suspect water according to the directions, and you'll have fairly safe water. Neither chlorine, nor any of these chemical methods will kill every possible microorganism, nor does it remove anything from the water. That's why you should also run the water through the best filtration you can afford.

I will admit that not having needed to yet, I haven't actually used any of these methods – it's all just "book knowledge", but I think that no matter which chemical method I use to kill the bugs, I'm still going to run all my water through filters. After all, I run my tap water through a filter now (just one of those water-pitcher filters), so why change old habits.

The needs of campers and hikers, humanitarian relief groups in the third world, and others with the need to have safe drinking water where it isn't readily available; they've all paved the way to come up with methods to ensure that water from natural sources is safe. There are great commercial filters available, as well as adequate homemade designs, which will filter out all but the littlest critters (and some even kill them.)

This is my plan: Water is freshly collected from the river in 5 to 7 gallon containers. I'd treat that water with bleach first. Before the water is used, or put into larger storage drums, I'd run it all through my Berkey filter system. Some of that water will later be used for boiling (for hot drinks and reconstituting freeze dried or dehydrated food) so by the time it's consumed, it's probably going to be the purest water I've ever had.

If you live in the desert, sure, it's beautiful out there, but I wonder where the water comes from. Do you have a well, or does the water make it to you by pipeline? Does a truck come and regularly refill a big tank? I'm sure you think about water much more than I do, so what could I tell you about the subject? At least you won't have wandering hordes of zombies coming by, at least not on foot.

Food

I've met a few people who eat for fuel, not for pleasure – they were serious bodybuilders. I can't get my head around that. I enjoy meals. After water and any medicines you must take, food is the next requirement.

I've heard that there are an awful lot of people who eat to just barely survive, and I know it's true because I've seen it on TV, but those are the billions of people who live in the third world. There are supposed to be people like that in the United States, but thanks to food pantries, soup kitchens, food stamps, and other government programs, I know the situation here can't be anything like the third world, where you're on your own, and the chances of actually starving to death is a real possibility. A starving third-worlder would give anything to be able to dumpster dive here in the United States to gather the food we throw away! If someone actually starved to death in this country, it would be on the news for days.

Being a middle class American, I've been insulated from such hardships all my life. Times may have gotten tight, my dad was out of work couple of times and there wasn't much money, but I've never gone hungry. Now, I can't imagine not being able to get anything I want to eat in a matter of minutes. Can I eat at Ruth's Chris Steakhouse every weekend? No, I can't afford that. Can I eat a steak from the supermarket every night? I probably could if I wanted to process all that red meat through my system every day, which I don't. Do I want to try to get through 6 months or a year of food shortage living on rice and beans? If I really had to, it has to beat starving, but I chose not to.

I say if you're going to go through the expense and effort of stocking up food for times of trouble, you might as well enjoy it. You're not going to have filet mignon and ice cream sundaes for desert, but whatever you stock up on, it'll be much more delicious than any alternatives will be if it ever comes to pass that you can't just go to the local supermarket anymore.

You can't live on grass soup – your stomach isn't built for it. Do you know what wild stuff is edible? Foraging for food is great in theory, but no matter how expert you are in picking edible mushrooms, leaves, nuts and berries, I'd bet you'll still starve to death, just more slowly. You need protein, so you'll have to do some hunting or trapping, too. I think I touched on this subject earlier. Is there much hunting in your neighborhood? You're probably going to have to drive to where the hunting is good. What if fuel isn't available? Who'll be protecting your family while you're off on a hunting trip? Bring the family with you, and you can cook and eat the deer you bag right on site, and drag the leftovers home. Hope your kids are fascinated watching you gut and clean Bambie. If it's so bad that you're going to have to hunt for food, what about the millions of other people doing the same thing? Unless you live in Montana or Alaska or some other sparsely populated area, not only will the population of deer and whatever else people hunt not last very long, but the woods will be filled with desperate amateur hunters blasting away at anything that moves. There might also be locals who might be blasting away at all the amateur hunters. Let's face it, successful hunting will be reserved for the few. It's not worth discussing here.

Your survival food pantry should contain a large amount of basic staples, such as rice and beans. You can also store various varieties of wheat, but wheat gets complicated.

If you know how to properly store and grind wheat to make flour to bake bread, you're probably wasting your time reading this; you know more about this subject than I do.

There are important rules for packing/preserving bulk foods, such as making sure it dry enough to prevent mold, and making sure there are no bug eggs and other things that can ruin those foodstuffs. I'll provide weblinks to sources of an incredible body of knowledge for that, but for me, I'm keeping it simple, and as I've said, this book is just an introduction to prepping. I'm still learning, and if you decide to get really serious, there's going to be so much more to learn than I'm able to teach.

I plan to have a pretty large quantity of stuff like rice and beans, but they'll have been professionally packaged for long-term storage, and they'll probably be used in a community type situation (running my own "soup kitchen" so to speak, for the unprepared neighbors).

Don't just get a bunch of 5 gallon plastic pails with covers, and think you can fill them up with rice or beans or whatever, and think you're good. Not only do you need food grade buckets (some plastics are not safe for food storage), but believe it or not, plastic buckets are not air-tight no matter how tightly the covers fit. Oxygen will actually slowly move through the plastic! I've seen it on YouTube. A guy had sealed some airtight buckets of rice and opened them up over 10 years later, and the white rice looked brown from oxidation. He packed it before he knew he had to line the buckets. You must line the buckets with mylar food bags (available at most preparedness stores), you must also put oxygen scavenger packets into the bags with your food, and seal the bags so they are airtight. These special mylar bags have a thin aluminum coating that will prevent oxygen from getting to the food.

Oxygen and moisture are the enemies of stored dry food. Heat is the enemy of all stored foods. All the big online prep stores will carry the buckets, the mylar bags, and the oxygen scavenger packs.

As I said, my plan is to have a community "stewpot" going, so the neighbors won't feel the need to murder me for my food. No, I'm not kidding. If I'm going to starve if my food is taken, I'll fight to the death to keep it, because taking my food will kill me, just slowly. Maybe there are people who would rather die of starvation than steal, but there are certainly people out there who will kill for a pair of designer sneakers. They will cut your throat to take your last dollar. If they're hungry, they'll certainly kill you for your food. If you are such a fool that you don't believe me, you must not have ever watched the news on TV, or read a newspaper. The world isn't populated by just nice, decent people.

Likewise I'd rather feed the neighbors a bowl of cereal and milk every morning and a bowl of beans and rice every evening than have to shoot them for the crime of being hungry like 95% of the other knuckleheads will be. They can also have all the water they need to drink; all they have to do is to go down to the river to collect water. I'll be able to make it safe to drink.

While there is no history in the US of anti-food hoarding laws, all it takes is a Presidential Executive Order. Contrary to rumor, I've done a LOT of research, and there is not at this time any law or order concerning individually stored foodstuffs, but there actually is one that says that if a state of emergency or martial law is declared, commercial and farm foodstuffs (along with any structures and equipment) can be collected by the government (for redistribution as they see fit, and they're really good at that). Guess who gets fed first? Of course, the important people - the government and the military! States can set their own laws about this, but if a national emergency is declared, it's within the realm of possibility that FEMA could be granted the power to confiscate and distribute any food hoards they encounter.

Well, things could get so bad that even though the government can make any fascist pronouncement they want to, there still may be no way for them to actually implement anything on an individual basis. I would imagine there was an awful lot of gold buried in backyards when, in the 1930's, the government made the private possession of over a small amount of gold illegal. They didn't send the army out to everyone's backyard with metal detectors (but if you stored your gold in safe deposit boxes at the bank, you were probably sunk.) We can't dwell on this, because if you aren't prepared, it won't matter anyway, will it? You'll be just one more person or family out of many millions who won't know where their next meal will be coming from. I'd rather have the food and worry about keeping it than not have food and worry about how to get some.

As far as my own personal menu goes, for breakfast, there's scrambled eggs already mixed with things like ham, bacon, peppers, onions etc. Thanks to a monthly sale at ww.BePrepared.com, I've got a few cans of freeze dried sausage "crumbles". That will go great with eggs for breakfast, pasta sauces, and some of it may even end up in a batch of rice and beans. I've got all sorts of cereals and granola (with the milk included) that comes with, or you can throw in, such goodies as blueberries, raspberries, or peaches; and let's not forget the "just add water" pancake mix varieties that will also get blueberries or raspberries tossed in, which reminds me to pick up a can or two of maple syrup if I can find it, or honey, which I know is available. I have a couple of cans of butter powder (which can be reconstituted as a

74

spread, but you can't cook with it), and I've already split a case of shelf-stable canned butter (which you can cook with) with some guys at work. I even have peanut butter powder. I'll miss bread, because I don't bake, but I've got plenty of crackers. For lunch and dinner there's more stuff than I can list from several manufacturers with various levels of cost and deliciousness.

If you want to buy one of those big food packages, which I highly discourage, check what they give you for breakfast. I just saw one that had only cereal for breakfast, every day, for a year. That'll get old fast. But it sure keeps the price down. Freeze dried scrambled eggs with bacon could cost you, let's see, I just checked – a single serving pouch is on sale at this moment for $4.50 as I write this (it's 320 calories.) A #10 can will set you back $32, which the label says contains 16 x 180 calorie servings. That's $2.00 a serving. Unfortunately, you'd need 10 meals a day to get the calories you need at that rate. I'd call it 9 x 320 calorie servings per can, which works out to $3.56 a serving. The cans aren't on sale at this time, or it would be even cheaper. But I can also add some sausage crumbles, and I can also have some hot or cold cereal with fruit, too. I can splurge on a great 500-600 calorie breakfast for five or six dollars, every once in a while, to break up the monotony of having cereal every day.

Storage

Can you prepare and store bulk food yourself? Certainly, many people can or jar their own home-grown vegetables and fruits, people even preserve their own meats. If you want to take this direction, you need to really know what you are doing. Improperly preserved foods can kill you, there are just so many things that can go wrong if you don't do it exactly right. Ever hear of botulism? You must get canning jars, make sure they are sterile, and prepare the food so it is sterile, get the food in the jar and seal it properly and get it 100% right. There are even home sealing machines for #10 cans.

I recommend either reading a book especially written about home canning, or have someone who knows how to do it help you. If you do preserve your own, try not to have a pantry filled with canned tomatoes. Tomatoes are fine, but they'll be tough to live on. I plan on having a wide variety of foods, and leaving all the preservation and packaging to the experts.

Before you go on a buying spree, you need to know where you're going to store all this food you're going to stockpile. You should always keep in mind one very important point – the cooler it is, the longer the food is going to last. Temperature, along with oxygen and humidity, is an enemy of shelf-life. A cool basement is better than a spare room upstairs. An air conditioned (in the summer) room or closet upstairs is a lot better than a garage. A warm garage beats a broiling attic. As a matter of fact, attics can get so hot on a sunny day, especially in the summer, that storing any food there is crazy talk. Attics are for storing stuff that is not affected by heat, and ALL food is affected by heat. You might want to throw stuff in the attic to make room for food elsewhere.

Maybe you need to be creative. You can sock away a lot in containers under the bed. You might have the bottom 2 or 3 feet of every closet available. If you have a big room, especially if you've turned your basement into a giant living room, you can line a wall with shelving (portable or permanent) and hang draperies in front of it, or even just drape sheets over it to make your storage less conspicuous (also less of an eyesore). You'd be amazed at the amount of storage you can have by lining a 10 or 12 foot wall with shelves. In the kitchen cupboards, you might pack away some useless space hogging non-food items to make more room for actual food.

If you live in an apartment, you'll have to be even more creative than if you had a whole house available. Perhaps, if you do live in an apartment, maybe mom and dad live in the area, and they won't mind if you stockpile your food at their place. It's a win-win situation. You'll have a place to bug out to, and they won't have to starve to death, which may be a fair exchange for putting up with you moving back in.

Only you know how much storage space you've got. You don't want to be the first Hoarder on a reality show because you can't move around in your home because it filled with food! Keep in mind, maybe nothing may happen for years. Maybe nothing will ever happen in your lifetime. We just don't know. Don't let preparedness take over your life. It should be a harmless hobby that might someday save your life, nothing more than that.

Whenever you buy food for your survival stocks, whether it be cans, MREs, boxes, pouches, buckets, whatever, you should use a magic marker to mark the month and year you bought them (or mark the suggested "best by" date. This way, you can rotate your stock by starting to eat this food as part of your daily life before they get too far beyond their "best by" date, and restock with newer stuff. The win-win of this method is that your food budget will only be slightly higher as you grow your surplus, and it will already be long ago paid for as you consume it. Food prices always go up, not down, so you're actually making an investment that will grow in value.

Your "excess" food, if there is such a thing, will be very useful in a barter situation, in case you decide to swap some food for toilet paper or other items you've forgotten or need more of. You can't eat money. You can't even get at your money if the banks are closed and the ATM machines aren't operating! Someone might be eager to swap a spare rifle and some ammunition for a week's worth of food, if they mostly stocked up on arms and not so much on food. Or maybe they have plenty of food, but didn't think to store coffee. Maybe they'd swap a can or two of food for a brick of coffee? Anything's possible, and anything useful will become very valuable when you can't just order more whenever you want to.

For food, I personally prefer the fully made freeze dried meals. I've got a lot of those 2 meal pouches, most of which only amount to one big meal for me, but I'm twice the size of some people (6'3", 240 lbs.) This takes up more room than #10 cans, but I have a lot of room. I've got a lot of #10 cans, too. Don't get me wrong, I'm not going to live on nothing but freeze dried. I've long ago jarred up a 25 lb. bag of Basmati rice (dry, in used but sterilized Mason Jars that spaghetti sauce came in, with oxygen scavenger packs.) Now, I'm starting to stock up on professionally packaged 5 gallon pails of rice and dry beans. I think that'll be the best bang for the buck to not only stretch out my "good stuff", but also serve as "charity" meals for the neighbors. Those buckets weigh 40 to 50 pounds, and cost about a dollar to two dollars a pound. They take up the least room I can imagine, considering how many meals they represent. Getting them professionally packaged with oxygen scavengers, they're good for at least 15 to 20 years or more, and each bucket represents hundreds of meals. In 10 years, you can buy a new bucket and donate the old one to a food bank.

In case you somehow have the wrong idea, I'm NOT talking about throwing thousands of dollars away down in your basement "just in case," and kissing it goodbye if nothing ever happens. This is all food that you can (and should) eat whenever you want to. There's such a thing as rotating your stock. You accumulate it over time, buying a lot and eating a little and let your reserves grow. The #10 can, properly packed, is supposed to be good for 15, 20, even 25 years or more, depending on what's in it – Mountain House knows for sure, they've been around long enough to be able to test their original batches.

In the interest of rotating your supply, you can start opening and eating a can every now and then, maybe in a decade or so. As long as you replace the plastic cover, the food will be good for a week or more. It'll last much longer if you can also put it in the refrigerator (if you're not in an event), where it is cold and dry. In addition to cans, they also make one, two, and four meal pouches. Pouches of Mountain House freeze dried food have been labeled as best eaten within 7 years, but stored in a cool place, it'll still be edible for years more than that. In fact, Mountain House recently released the results of a taste test that showed that pouches of some meals can still taste good after 30 years!

Some companies advertise that their pouches are good for that 20 year mark depending on the brand and whether they're lying or not (any growing industry is going to attract scammers – there are very few source manufacturers, everyone else is a reseller or re-brander.) Some brands, you pour hot water right into the pouch, other brands, you empty their pouches into the hot water. I don't want to get too far into specific foods here, suffice it to say there's quite a variety as more players enter the market, and like anything else, some people like Pepsi, others like Coke, and the rest prefer 7-Up, or Mountain Dew, Orange Soda, or Iced Tea.

As an introduction to freeze dried meals, and what I'm sure they considered to be "an ordeal to go through just to humor the nutty neighbor" (considering how long it took me to get them to sit still for it), I recently treated my next door neighbors to a meal of freeze dried Mountain House Lasagna, Mountain House Turkey Tetrazzini (tastes like a Turkey Pot Pie without the crust,) with Alpine Aire Green Beans Almandine and Mountain House Raspberry – Chocolate Crumble Dessert poured over reconstituted peach chunks (and some fresh black raspberries from my own patch, since they're in season.) They LOVED it! They could hardly believe it was freeze dried, but they're converts now.

I doubt if they're going to do any stocking up, I don't know if they care enough, but if the time ever comes, at least I'll have them to help with security and fetching water, and they'll already know that delicious meals await them. One of the Preppers at work recently introduced Mountain House food to his family – wife and 3 young children. They had Lasagna, Teriyaki Chicken, and Peaches with Raspberry – Chocolate Crumble dessert, and they all loved it. When a picky 4 year old says "dad, this emergency food is good!" you know it'll compete with McDonalds any day.

If you do as I do, and order a couple hundred dollars' worth of food and gear two or three or four times a year, or whatever you can afford, and pick up a case or so of cans at the supermarket when they're on sale, you'll eventually have quite a comfortable supply, even as you occasionally prepare meals out of your stocks (I can't stress this enough - you'd better – I'd imagine it would suck to find out you bought a lot of something you can't stand, and not a lot of what you love - that's why I'm against starting out by buying those giant package deals). You could buy less, but you'll be paying a lot more money for shipping that way.

Many companies have a flat shipping rate, or at least a maximum, in fact some offer free shipping if you buy over a certain dollar value, so it's cheaper overall to make fewer, but higher value purchases. Some also offer better deals for larger quantities, which is another advantage of talking to people and finding other Preppers. Be Prepared has deals every month at close to half price if you meet minimum purchase requirement. Splitting the order with others makes this a great deal.

Have you ever heard the term "dollar cost averaging"? In the investing world, it means buying a set dollar amount of a stock on a regular basis – if the price is high, you get fewer shares, and if the price is low, you get more shares. Well, I like to think of food storage in much the same way, but based on shelf life. If you go out and buy $1,000 worth of something in one shot, when it expires (whether it be a couple of years or a couple of decades) you'll need to get rid of or use all of it, and replace that whole batch. If you get a reasonable amount on a regular basis, then there will be a much smaller quantity to use as the food approaches its shelf-life. Some items, like cans, should **never** be thrown out as long as the can is in good shape – it might not taste great, but it will keep you alive. Canned food can be edible and still maintain some nutritional value for 100 years! Other items, like powdered milk, actually goes bad (discoloration and clumping are clues, bad taste is the clincher). Not bad as in, if you drink it you'll die, more like, if you drink it, it tastes horrible, and the nutritional benefits are so low, why bother?

Even if you're not rich like me, you should at least build up some kind of reserve by buying extras of the appropriate (long shelf life) items as you do your regular food shopping. Cans of chunky soup, cans of tuna or chicken, corn, beans, Spam, whatever you LIKE and eat anyway. If you can't even afford that, well, I'm so sorry. You probably blow $7 a day on cigarettes. I feel for you but I can't reach you.

MREs

You might get by with MREs (Meals, Ready to Eat) for a few days. They have a shelf life anywhere from a few years to much more – like all food items; it all depends on the temperature they're stored at. There have been lots of studies done by the government. There have been all sorts of interpretations of government data. Basically, the MRE is designed to last around 3 years stored at 80 degrees, but their own testing says that the taste and nutritional value is "acceptable" when stored twice that long. If you put in into a 120 degree attic, just one month up there will ruin them (1 month shelf life). If you keep it in a 60 degree basement, it'll be good for well over 10 years. Figure that if they haven't been in a warehouse out in the desert or in an attic for any length of time, and you keep them at room temperature, they should be good for 5 to 7 years, which is pretty much the minimum for freeze-dried pouch foods.

MREs are pretty popular, but I haven't had the pleasure of eating any. My military duty was from 1974 to 1980, preceding the introduction of the modern MRE. I think I recall eating K-Rations a few times, I say I think because they weren't memorable meals, or at least there weren't any good memories of them, and the brain tends to want to ignore bad memories if it can.

C-rations, K-rations, or MREs, none were meant to be consumed long-term, it was always to be used temporarily, during combat. The military definition of temporary is loosely defined as around 10 days for MREs, although they have been used far longer by some unfortunate souls. For my temporary survival situation, my definition of temporary far surpasses 10 days. No way am I going to try to survive on MREs. They're great for bug-out bags, and you might want to have some around for convenience, as the preparation requirements are minimal, but anyone who thinks it's a good idea to put away a large quantity of these is not going to be enjoying their choice for long. There are anecdotal stories about very negative side effects of MREs. They are very low in fiber and very high in salt. They supposedly will cause serious constipation.

If you've already bought yourself a big box of them, well, they are food, and can be used for charity – beggars can't be choosers. Keep an eye on the expiration date (if you can figure it out, I've read that they use that weird Julian-type dating method where the first digit is the year, the next 3 digits is the day of the year out of 365.) So 3001 would be Jan 1, 2003. Or is it 1993? Some companies use 2 digits for the year, which is much more helpful for this application. Anyway, they stopped allowing civilian sales of real military MRE's years ago due to too much theft, so if you have real military MREs, unless they've been stored in a relatively cool place, they may already be too old to taste right, nor provide some of the nutrients.

You can be sure that if they are real military MREs, they're extremely old, or maybe they're freshly stolen. If it says "not for civilian sale," they are newer, but it's been stolen from the government, too, and they could still already be many years old. Plus, you don't know how they were stored before you got them. Were they sitting in a warehouse in Arizona in the baking heat for a few years?

The companies that make them started making a civilian version of the MRE – same production line, just less choices and some other differences that aren't significant to you, like spoon size, and some differences that might be significant, like smaller portion size. You can buy them through reputable resellers, and expect them to taste fine for five to ten years as long as they're stored in a cool enough place, like a basement (60-70 degrees). They also aren't so much cheaper than the better choices for meals that if you've got them already, fine, but if you don't, only get a limited supply if at all.

Fortunately, you don't have to buy whole MRE packages. Plenty of distributors allow you to buy the individual components. From what I've read, their deserts are pretty good. There are items such as Fudge Brownies, a few varieties of Pound Cakes, Lemon and Almond Poppy seed Cakes, Apple Turnovers, Chocolate Chip and Oatmeal Cookies, a few varieties of applesauce, etc. These would be a heck of a lot better than no snacks at all, and they're around a dollar or two each.

I believe this article will tell you everything you ever wanted to know about MREs:

www.millennium-ark.net/News_Files/Food/MREs

Canned Food

Probably the smartest and least expensive thing you can do is to start, this very week, stocking up on canned food from grocery or warehouse stores. There's no end to the varieties of canned food, and while I've heard that for some foods, fresh and frozen may taste better and supposedly retain more nutritional value, we are talking about a time when you can't just go to the supermarket to buy frozen food anyway, so it doesn't really matter, does it?

Keep in mind that you need carbohydrates, protein, and not too much fat and salt. You can look on the label and make your choices – proteins are usually more expensive than carbs, so make sure there's enough protein in those cans. You're not going to stay too healthy living on canned corn alone. There are also lots of canned meats, from Spam to real Hams, tuna, chicken; I even scored a case of salmon.

Don't forget the fiber! If you drastically change your eating habits in a small amount of time, it's going to take some getting used to. One thing you don't want to deal with is, let's say, being "blocked up!"

You might want to have some spices to add for flavor, and if you're a cooking type of person, you can even do things like salmon croquets, even tuna casseroles.

You may be out of luck when it comes to mayonnaise, but maybe not – if you have a packet of dry egg whites (don't buy any till you hear about OvaEasy!) and salad oil (some oils will last a long time if kept airtight) and one of those old fashioned egg beaters (where you turn the crank and the beaters counter-rotate) you can probably beat yourself a fair approximation of mayonnaise whenever you want to. Only make as much as you can use if there's no power. Unless it's winter, that would solve the problem with refrigeration. Throw some snow in a cooler and you're set for a while.

I don't know anyone who uses a lot of canned foods these days, but you can always make a decent meal out of a can of chunky soup, or a few cans of different items – let's say a can of tuna, corn, and peas, just like when you (hopefully) have a balanced meal now - there's a protein, a vegetable, and a "starch". What I'm getting at, without playing nutritionist (because I certainly don't have that qualification), is to tell you to keep a balance in your stockpile, so you can have balanced meals. It would be better to get one case of meat and one case of corn, than to get two cases of corn. Next time, do it again, but with different stuff.

You can live for days on chips and beer, but I doubt if you can do it for months without causing health problems. Nutritional deficiencies creep up on you, but they can be debilitating. In the old days, sailors used to get scurvy due to the lack of vitamin C. All I know about scurvy is that I don't want to get it. Cans of citrus fruits or fruit juices will get you some vitamin C. Acidic products will probably eat into the can over time, so citrus and tomato sauce cans won't last as long as non-acidic foods, but they usually coat the insides of food cans based on the content. I'd bet that cans of orange juice or pineapple juice are still drinkable a year or two past their "best by" date, which is already at least a year. You will definitely know if it is no longer palatable by the smell when you open it. If you open a can and it's fine in a year, maybe you'll want to polish off that case and replace it with a fresh one. If it's already hit the fan, unless you're a real juice fanatic, you'll probably go through what you've got before nature takes it from you. You really should have a lot of powdered stuff, like Tang, so you can have a dependable source of C for a long time.

You can always keep up a stock of vitamins. The big outlets like Costco, Sams, and BJs have mega-sized containers, and the expiration date is usually a couple of years out. Instead of having one container, then replacing it when you get to the bottom, have one sealed one and one you're using. When you get to the bottom of the open one, go buy a fresh one, but put that one on the shelf and start using your backup one. That's how you rotate.

On most canned foods, the use-by date or expiration date is a suggestion and/or a government requirement, not necessarily based on any science at all.

The truth is that cans that have been properly manufactured, and all major food companies do that right, have no dents (botulism!)that can possibly compromise them can be eaten much longer than the government required expiration date. A lot of expiration dates are more like "best by" dates. From all I've read, the first thing to go is taste, and then some nutritional loss. Yes, if the food is old, but it isn't compromised by mold or some other rot, it may not taste as good, and it have lost a lot of some nutrients, but it's not going to kill you. It won't keep you alive as long as good, properly stored food within its shelf life. If the packaging is compromised even the tiniest bit, toss it – there's nothing you can do with it. If a can looks "swollen" - toss it. If it has a bad smell when you open it – toss it.

A properly packaged can that is in good shape can conceivable be edible for decades or longer. In 1968, a 100 year old ship was found that had a cache of assorted canned foods. Some of the food was eventually sent to be analyzed, and it turns out it was all not only edible, but still had some nutritional value.

From the Hormel website:

"What is the shelf life of a Hormel Foods product in an unopened can?

The processing techniques utilized by Hormel Foods makes the canned product safe for use indefinitely if the product seal remains intact, unbroken and securely attached to a can that has been well maintained. It is suggested that all canned products be stored in a cool and dry environment to keep the flavor adequately preserved. For maximum flavor it is recommended that the product be used within three years of the manufacturing date. After that period of time, the product is still safe to use however, the flavor gradually declines."

The Bertrand was a 100 year old shipwreck that was recovered, and they found a horde of canned food on it.

From FDA Consumer Magazine in the article The Canning Process: Old Preservation Technique Goes Modern:

"Among the canned food items retrieved from the Bertrand in 1968 were brandied peaches, oysters, plum tomatoes, honey, and mixed vegetables. In 1974, chemists at the National Food Processors Association (NFPA) analyzed the products for bacterial contamination and nutrient value. Although the food had lost its fresh smell and appearance, the NFPA chemists detected no microbial growth and determined that the foods were as safe to eat as they had been when canned more than 100 years earlier. The nutrient values varied depending upon the product and nutrient. NFPA chemists Janet Dudek and Edgar Elkins report that significant amounts of vitamins C and A were lost. But protein levels remained high, and all calcium values 'were comparable to today's products. and

"NFPA chemists also analyzed a 40-year-old can of corn found in the basement of a home in California. Again, the canning process had kept the corn safe from contaminants and from much nutrient loss. In addition, Dudek says, the kernels looked and smelled like recently canned corn."

Do you like Campbells Chunky Soups? Try all the varieties, and the ones you like should be added to your stock. Get some beef based, chicken based, and whatever else suits your fancy. How about Chef Boyardee, they have several pasta with meat combinations you may like. You don't want to be eating the same thing day after day. Whenever they're on sale, buy a lot of them. Do you like canned tuna? Canned chicken? Corn, peas, you name it. Maybe you don't.

Try an experiment. Every time you see something canned on sale, get one to try, and if you find it edible, then go back and get a bunch.

Over time (measured in years) you may accumulate enough that you'll be able to start eating the older stuff (rotate your stock.) You don't have to eat nothing but cans for every meal, but you can certainly add a few cans to your weekly menu to use the stuff up.

If you end up with a years' worth of canned goods on shelves in the cellar or in a closet in a spare room, then you will be a winner if you suddenly find that you can't get any more cans, or anything else for that matter. I'd count shelf-stable meals, like from Hormel, to be in the can category. The important thing is that they don't need refrigeration, and because the whole point of the exercise is that there's no electricity, the first stuff you'll eat before it rots is the stuff in your freezer and refrigerator. There goes the first week.

Oh, yeah - don't forget your can opener! Or your backup can opener! If you have one of those side cutting can openers, keep in mind that cans that come with plastic lids (like most #10 cans) need the lip of the can to hold them closed. If you use a side-cutter instead of a top-cutter, it cuts off the lip, so the lid won't have anything to grab, so only use side-cutters on "single serving" cans.

Freeze Dried

Thanks to hikers, backpackers, and oddly enough, the Church of Jesus Christ of Latter Day Saints (the Mormons) who are wisely advised to make sure they are prepared to be self-sufficient, an industry of long-term survival food has developed. Far beyond the old fashioned canned foods is a wealth of all sorts of shelf stable food products and complete meals good for many years, if not decades! Most amazing is the freeze-drying process. If that's new to you, go to their websites and read about it. Basically, they freeze fresh food or freshly cooked recipes, and put the food into vacuum chambers where the frozen water is evaporated without turning liquid again. In case you were absent that day in science class, the process is called sublimation. Unlike dehydrated food that shrinks, freeze dried foods maintain their size and texture. They are rehydrated with boiling, or even room temperature water. Green beans will still be crispy, and lasagna will be delicious, with stringy cheese, too. I can vouch for that.

The largest company of them all is Oregon Freeze Dry who freeze-dry food for their own label, Mountain House www.mountainhouse.com 1-800-547-0244, as well as other companies' food labels, and have product lines that make components that other food companies add to their own products (like the bits of fruit they add to breakfast cereals, etc.) They also do big freeze drying jobs for the government. They even have a couple of factories in Europe. If you want to, and have enough money, you can probably have them freeze dry whatever you want to pay them to. They aren't the only ones, though, and you may want to get some food from an assortment of manufacturers and retail dealers. By the way, Oregon Free Dry will sell you their products retail direct, but they protect their established resellers by not discounting the price. Many manufacturers do the same. So while they maintain their suggested retail pricing, the resellers are free to run sales if they want to, so it pays to shop around, for each and every purchase. Or do as I do, wait till something you want is on sale and stock up.

It's hard to get a read on exactly who makes what for whom, though.

There's Alpine Aire (www.alpineaire.com (406) 585-9324), another company that sells a line of freeze-dried foods. I don't know if Alpine Aire does the freeze drying themselves or have another company do it, but their food is definitely not the same as Mountain House. Actually, I know nothing at all about them except that it's marketed by a company called Infinet Communications, Inc. 8551 Cottonwood Rd., Bozeman, MT 59718.

I've personally tried a lot of Alpine Aire, meals, which I find overall to be more like what I consider "health" food, heavier in grains and lighter in bold flavors. To be fair, they're probably targeted more at healthy, "outdoorsy" people, as opposed to couch potatoes like me. A lot of their meals are also lighter in animal proteins than I'd prefer. Their meat based dinners seem to me to be much lighter on the meat than Mountain House. Then again, they seem to specialize in Gluten Free meals, and they have a lot of items that other companies don't, they even have freeze dried dog food! They've been around a long time, so don't go by my taste buds. I've also tried a lot of Mountain

House meals, which are some of my personal favorites. But I'm not going to go through a list of all the meals available and tell you what I like and don't like. That's for you to do, as I did.

Buy an assortment of meals from different companies, do a taste test yourself, or especially with your family, and maybe some like-minded friends, and then you'll know what you like and what to stock up on. Alpine Aire also sells a changing assortment of survival equipment and supplies on their website, like canning machines, survival matches stored in #10 cans, cans of Alaskan Salmon, and whatever else suits their fancy. It's a good site to visit on occasion just to see what they've got.

I will say that I've seen a few big name survival food companies who have some products that look suspiciously like Mountain House products. Keep in mind, Oregon Freeze Dry is in the business of manufacturing, and like any manufacturer, they are always looking for customers. If you have the money, and want to start your own company, I'm sure they would be happy to package any product line you want to pay them for, and slap your label on the can or pack it into your pouches. If you then sell the product for double what others charge, maybe because you have a huge advertising budget, that's your right.

Again, if you decide that all or part of your food supply will be freeze dried meals, please do your own taste test! Do it before sinking possibly thousands of dollars into any companies' giant package deals. Get a variety of meal pouches from different manufacturers and see which ones you like. They're usually one or two person, sometimes 4 person meals, and cost in the neighborhood of $6 to $10 per pouch (or much less if you catch a sale). Then order a lot more of what you liked, both the pouches and if available, the #10 cans.

A few of tips on that:

Like any other products sold by competitors, the resellers can run sales, so if you keep your eyes open you may find deals on what you like for 10%, 20%, even 30% off. I found an incredible deal once at my local Costco – a variety pack of 10 Mountain House two-person meal pouches for only $39.99, or $4 per pouch ($2 per serving). That's less than a fast food burger! Three of us at work bought 10 boxes each.

It usually costs less per meal for pouches than the #10 cans (although the pouches have an advertised "best before" life of 5 to 7 years, and the cans are more like 20-30 years, take up less room, and protect the food better.

When you prepare the food, use a bit LESS water than the directions tell you to. If they say add two cups of boiling water, start with only a cup and a half. Stir it up, reseal and let it sit for the 10 or 12 minutes recommended. When you reopen the pack, give it another good stirring. If it seems too dry, you can always add a little bit more hot water, stir, and let sit another 5 minutes. It's harder to remove excess water – if you pour off the excess liquid, you lose some of the sauce. I don't understand how these companies think that turning most of their meals into soups will make it seem like you're getting more food. It's the same number of calories per package. Almost every pouch I've ever tried comes out better using less than the recommended amount of water.

Of course, there are also companies like Wise that have pouches that you pour into the boiling water, instead of adding water to the pouch. You can still use less water, but you'll need another pot with some boiling water in it to make the consistency the way you like it. I've only tried one Wise free sample 4 person pouch (pasta in a creamy cheese sauce.) It tasted okay for a pot of noodles with sauce – but that's all it was, noodles & sauce. Everyone who tried it thought the taste was acceptable. If you want meat in it, you pay extra by using a meat pouch, and their meat portions are miniscule, so they're very expensive. If you want vegetables in it, you have to add that too. By the time you're done, it's become a very expensive meal. Of course you can get the main dishes from them, and then add freeze dried chicken, or beef, or meatballs from a different company. You'll end up with more meat in your meal for a much lower price. You can add vegetables the same way. When you buy the Wise brand buckets of vegetables pouches or their buckets of fruit pouches, you're also getting a bunch of pouches of different sauces. Overall, they might taste pretty good, but I think it's an expensive way to go. You can't buy individual pouches (as of now), and as I said, if you want fruits or vegetables, inside the bucket you're getting a bunch of high "empty" calorie sauces with it whether you like it or not. These sauces are cheap for them, making the overall food system that much more expensive for you.

Being suspicious of the Wise Foods claim of a 25 year shelf life for their pouches, Mountain House foods paid for a scientific analysis of Wise Foods. The analysis was made public in June, 2012. The result was that the atmosphere inside the Wise packages had almost the same oxygen content as, well, air. It was over 100 times more oxygen than in the Mountain House packages that were also tested and for which Mountain House only claims a 7 year shelf life! Bottom line – Wise foods can have nowhere near the shelf life they claim, but you may not know it until you open the packages to find spoiled food. This, plus the absurd cost structure of Wise, makes me want to warn you that just because a company pays big bucks for star endorsement doesn't mean it is a good deal for you. Especially if you give them thousands of dollars, store a load of their buckets of pouches in the cellar, and then perhaps 10 years later, need that food only to find out most of it went bad, and what's left are tiny "servings".

"ALBANY, Ore. – July 12, 2012 – Mountain House, the leading domestic brand of freeze-dried food, released the results today of a study designed to illustrate how different brands handle oxygen levels in their long-term food storage products. The study, conducted by Columbia Food Laboratories, focused on oxygen levels found in pouches of Mountain House freeze-dried foods compared to those of a competitor.

"For proper long-term food storage, it's important to maintain oxygen exposure as low as possible," said Lee Goin, laboratory director at Columbia Food Laboratories. "Oxygen causes rancidity in foods containing unsaturated fats. Even slight rancidity can make a food undesirable. Oxygen causes nutritional value to be lost, especially vitamins A, C, D and E. Removal of oxygen will kill any insects, larvae and their eggs that may to be present."

Consumers should be aware that there are four main contributors to food spoilage: water, heat, light, and oxygen. Freeze drying removes 98% of the water in food, while dehydrating removes between 80% and 97%. Storing food in a cool, dark place helps to avoid heat and light exposure. However, the fourth factor, oxygen, can only be averted through quality processing and packaging, which is where the study found competitor's products falling short.

"Our curiosity was piqued when we saw brands such as Wise Company implying that their pouches have up to a 25-year shelf life, which is rarely found in pouches of freeze-dried foods," commented Norm Jager, head of research and development for Mountain House. "Freeze-dried meals serve families in times of dire need when emergencies hit, which means that it's imperative that these foods deliver on the promises made. So instead of just sitting on the sidelines, we decided to test their products in an effort to educate consumers across the U.S. on the importance of oxygen, which should ideally be less than 2 percent for long term food storage."

Oxygen Levels in Wise Company Products were 110 Times Higher Than Mountain House Mountain House commissioned Columbia Food Laboratories to test 30 samples of dehydrated and freeze dried meals from Wise Company as well as 30 samples of comparable Mountain House freeze dried meals. The results were staggering. Average oxygen levels in Wise Company products were 18.25%, nearly the 21% level found in the atmosphere and 110 times higher than the average 0.16% oxygen found in Mountain House products. The most alarming part is that Wise Company products were manufactured in April of 2012 and already exhibit near-atmospheric levels of oxygen, which would not provide a 25-year shelf life.

In distinction, Mountain House has a long-standing history of excellence in the freeze-dried foods industry, pioneering the necessary technology and processes for more than 40 years. As part of a rigorous, ongoing quality assurance program, Mountain House regularly tests its own archived products from as far back as 35 years."

Wise Foods responded to these charges, without actually denying the facts. Note that they don't actually say how much oxygen is in their pouches, and they say their pouches are "capable" of lasting 25 years, not that they actually do. Wise has no real, experimental basis for their contention that their foods will last for the time they claim, as they've only been in business a few years. Additionally, I've seen retailers on blogs claim to have stopped carrying Wise products due to finding Wise pouches that have already gone bad.

"Salt Lake City, Utah – July 16, 2012: Mountain House, a supplier of emergency and outdoor foods, issued a press release on July 12, 2012 targeting a single competitor: Wise Company. Why attack Wise Company when Mountain House has dozens of other competitors? Because Mountain House is now launching a new bucket and pouch line designed for emergency preparedness very similar to a product that has been a specialty of Wise Company since their inception.

Wise Company has experienced tremendous growth over the last few years with its emergency foods packaged in pouches capable of lasting up to 25 years. During this time, Mountain House has claimed that food pouches have no more than a 7-year shelf life. Now, in conjunction with the launch of its new product line, Mountain House has changed its story and claims that pouches can achieve a 25-year shelf life!

Wise Company takes great pride in providing high quality emergency food with a long-term shelf life. The Mountain House surprise attack relies on a lab study commissioned and presumably paid for by Mountain House. Notably, Wise Company's existing quality testing and data show oxygen levels in its products lower than those alleged by Mountain House. Wise Company's raw materials and finished goods contain very low moisture levels. The extreme low moisture content contributes to product stability. Wise Company product is then packed in ultra-high barrier (UHB) packaging with a very low oxygen transmission rate as well as a very low water vapor transmission rate (WTR). Once sealed, Wise individual pouches are stored in durable plastic containers. These elements, along with proper storage and temperature, are essential to providing consumers with quality products capable of lasting up to 25 years.

"We take our obligations in this industry very seriously," said Brian Neville, president and CEO of Wise Company. "We have confidence in our food pouches standing the test of time."

Once you have your supplies, you can be as inventive as you want to be with them. A #10 can is usually an average of 10 meals, but you don't have to eat it all till it's gone. If you put the plastic cover back on the can, it'll last for several days. It could even last for weeks or more depending on what it is. Because the product is freeze dried, it is very dry, and as long as you keep it dry it is good to go. Once it starts absorbing moisture from the air, it's time to use it all up. I keep a can of dehydrated peaches in my refrigerator. I use it as dessert, snack, and with breakfast cereal. It's stays good and dry in the refrigerator. I've also as an experiment, left some out on the kitchen counter. It was still edible the next day, but the day after that, it had started to absorb water from the air, and started feeling stick. At that point, I felt it really wasn't edible anymore. The stuff in the closed can in the refrigerator is still good many weeks later.

I tend to buy a lot of my food from Emergency Essentials (www.beprepared.com) which not only resells Mountain House, but also has their own house brand of dehydrated and freeze dried foods called Provident Pantry. Whatever Mountain House doesn't make, the Provident Pantry label seems to make up for, like fruits, vegetables, cereals, grains, and single item cans of meats like chicken, which you can't ever have too much of.

NitroPak (www.nitropak.com) is another large preparation supply house. They carry the Mountain House line, and put it on sale from time to time, as well as carry a great deal of other survival supplies and equipment.

No matter what the company, be cautious about making large package purchases. There are some food supply companies out there, selling what I would call "future regret food packages" (because by the time you realize you've been snookered, it'll be way too late). It's rare enough that people will decide to prepare, but when they do, they shouldn't be ripped off.

These companies sell all sorts of great sounding package deals, claiming "lowest prices", have fancy packaging and fancy websites, but sell food based on the number of servings (whatever that means to them) versus the number of calories per day. Even with a high calorie count, be sure it's not because they're including a bunch of cans of "drink mixes" consisting of sugar and flavoring and not much more. Any drink mix should at least be fortified with some nutrients. Empty calories from sugar are the cheapest way for them to inflate their calorie claims. I'm not saying that their food is not good edible food, they can't legally sell "bad" food in the US, and it would only take one person to turn them into the authorities to shut them down or get them prosecuted criminally. What I'm saying is that they are selling you a lot less food than they are trying to make you believe you're getting.

When you look carefully at the nutritional labels and do the math, you'll find that some of these package deals would be considered insufficient for people who are on weight-loss diets! Unless you eat 10 of their "meals" a day, it isn't going to be enough food. I've seen them take a package containing 2 decent meals, and call it 4 meals. I've even seen 6 meals! I've seen crooks who have the nerve to call 100 calories a meal! They also may pad their packages with a lot of soup mixes that they consider meals (most people add a cup of soup to a meal, not call it THE meal! Yes, some soups are so hearty and full of meats and vegetables that they ARE meals, but a cup of tomato soup surely isn't a meal!) You'll also find, as with Wise, that sometimes their promises of how long their food will last might be wildly inflated.

Bottom line - their overall packages do not supply enough nutrition to keep you healthy for anywhere near as long as advertised. They don't care. They'll have made their money, and once you need to start using your emergency food, it'll be far too late to do anything about it. You'll have paid for a 6 month supply and ended up without enough food to get through 3 months, if that. I can't mention any names, because unless I do a lot of nutritional calculations (if I can even get the data, and the labeling can change constantly) and send their food out to an independent lab for analysis, they're going to sue my pants off. All I can do is warn you that they exist, and tell you "buyer beware". My conclusion on all of them is that if you can't buy a sample of each and every item they sell, and they don't prominently display their nutritional information including what they consider to be a serving, they are charlatans and you'd do better not to waste your money.

Rotation

This is the term used to describe how, even as you add to your food stockpile, you should know how old your existing foods are, and use your stored foods before they get too old. Once you've been adding to your storage for a while, you should start using up the oldest containers and replace what you use (or even accumulate more), so you won't have to ever throw away food that is too old. This has the advantage of getting you and your family used to eating the foods you are storing.

There's a company that sells expensive shelving units, where you put the newest cans on a canted shelf, and they roll back and around to the next lower shelf by gravity. On the lower section, the first can in line is the oldest; the newest can will be the first one on the upper section. As you add more to the upper shelf and use the cans on the lower shelf, they keep rolling down. So you when you need something, you grab the first can in line and the rest will roll down one notch after you pull the can. The shelves cost up to hundreds of dollars. It's a neat system; it comes in different sized shelves for different sized cans, and if you want them and can afford them, go ahead and get them. They're merely a convenience.

I use assemble-yourself (no tools needed) plastic shelves from Home Depot that cost around $30-40, and I can figure out how to put the new stuff behind the old stuff without having to invest a ton of money on fancy shelf systems, thank you very much.

If you are storing, say, Silk Soy Milk because you're lactose intolerant, and you've accumulated several months supply of the stuff, as you buy more, you should use the oldest containers in storage first and put the new stuff away. This way, whenever there's an event, you'll always have a fresh supply in storage. If you're storing 20-30 year shelf life cans, you can still eat some, but you'll never accumulate a 20 year supply (unless you've got a ton of room and can spend a ton of bucks) so you won't have to worry so much about consuming it before it goes bad.

You should date mark everything (either packages or individual cans) with an easy to read permanent marker (just to make it easier to read later) as you get it and put it in storage. What date to use? Either when you got it, or when you need to use it by. More on this in a little bit. I once brought an old bottle of powdered non-dairy creamer to work to use in my coffee. It had expired a few years earlier. People who noticed the date freaked out, like I had poison! It still worked fine, for powdered coffee whitener.

You can mark your purchase date, although that doesn't mean it hasn't been sitting on a store shelf or in a warehouse for who knows how long. A can or other package could have been sitting around for weeks, months, even years by the time you buy it.

Sometimes the "made on" date is on the package. If it's not clearly labeled (and it usually isn't), it may be in code. The usual code is a five digit number. The first two digits are for the year, and the next three digits are the day of the year (running from 1 to 365). 05365 would be the last day of 2005; 11001 would be Jan. 1, 2011. If you can't figure it out, you can contact the manufacturer, either by phone or email. It might show what the codes mean somewhere on their website. I know Mountain House does that. They've even changed the code over the years.

You can mark the manufacturers best-by or expiration date printed on the can or package, if there is one. If there's no "best-by" date clearly printed on the package, then you have to use your best judgment. As we already know, a can may have a use-by date on it, but that would just be a suggestion, at best.

The problem with the use-by date is that just because the manufacturer has to follow some government determined table of shelf lives, it could be totally bogus (I've seen an expiration date on a package of table salt (and it wasn't in the millions of years)! Remember, the government is there to help you. A can of corn might best be used within two or three years, but it will be perfectly fine in five years, and it might still be edible in 50-100 years.

Mountain House did a taste test in June 2012 of some of their 7 year shelf life freeze dried meal pouches. They compared freshly made pouches with pouches that have been stored for at least 30 years.

That's THIRTY years. Although they didn't do a nutritional analysis, as far as taste went, the results were astounding. On a 1-9 "Hedonic Scale" (Google that!), the fresh stuff scored 8.5-8.6 (Like Very Much to Like Extremely), and the old stuff averaged 6.6 (Like Slightly to Like Moderately). Some people rated Beef Stew and Rice and Chicken a 9 (Like Extremely), both for the new batch and the old batch). The point is that if you have a pouch of Mountain House that is 10 years old and it says it's past its "use-by" date, don't throw it out, eat it. If it doesn't taste good, then throw it out. It's not going to be bad or harmful for you. If sealed food goes bad, usually cans and pouches will swell from the gasses the microorganisms produce. If you open a container of any kind, make sure you or someone with a working nose smells it. If it is bad, it normally will smell bad. That goes for food you just got from the store, as well as the stuff you've had stored in the cupboard for years.

You really need to decide for yourself how long you're willing to store an item based on what it is and the temperature of your storage area, and mark down your own best-by date.

Whatever method you decide to use, just keep in mind the point of the exercise – you want to know when you'll need to consume the can or other package before it's too old to taste good. Just because a food package is "too old", as long as it isn't spoiled and harmful, it might not taste as good as it should, and it may have lost a good amount of its nutritional use, it's still food and it will still beat starving to death.

Pets

I don't mean the pets ARE food. Well, they could be, depends on how bad things get. I just wanted to remind you, don't forget the pet food, folks. In case of an event, you probably should be able to keep feeding your pets too, don't you think? I think a dog is well worth feeding, they're great for early warning, and if they're big enough, they may be helpful for defense. Cats? Well, if they'll make you feel better…

I'm not a veterinarian, but I don't think you can feed your pets rice and beans. Well, you could, but just until they die. So try to properly store lots of dry pet food, hopefully the kind they eat anyway. I know there are commercially packaged emergency foods available for pets, and I bet it'll get even more widely available as more people look for the stuff, but not being a pet owner, I delegate that task to you.

You can also put away as much food in the way of cans as you can afford, too. Canned dog and cat food is probably going to have a similar shelf life as people food – almost indefinite. Um, do you keep rabbits? Sorry, cute they may be, but THEY are food.

Here's a few online pet food store that sells of freeze dried pet foods. There are numerous others, do a Google search.

www.onlynaturalpet.com   www.bellaspainrelief.com
www.stevesrealfood.com

The reason they're freeze dried is because they use raw meats in the ingredients. Also some are organ meats. It's difficult stuff for a manufacturer to handle. If not freeze dried, it would have to be handled frozen, which increases the costs a lot. If you think your pet is a little human, you aren't being kind, not to their digestive systems, anyway. Experts agree that cats and dogs do just fine on meat products that you and I consider disgusting. Only one thing to do, read up and try them out.

From what I've read, you'll need to switch your pet to these foods for a while to see if they agree with them. No need to invest in something that at some point you find out that your pet won't eat.

Staples

You might think the staple foods of the American diet are hamburgers and pizza. By definition, staples are what a population eats a lot of on a regular basis. Actually, our staples are more like wheat (bread & pasta,) cereal, beans, potatoes, rice and corn. Then there's "dairy" (eggs, milk, and cheese) too. Being a melting pot, America probably has the widest definition of "staple foods" in the world. Maybe include meat; we Americans eat more meat than elsewhere in the world (most likely because it's cheap and plentiful here).

Some of us eat too much. What if the time comes when we're more like the developing world, with a food supply that doesn't meet our needs? The recent droughts affecting much of the country are already making the price of many foods skyrocket. For a temporary, but lengthy interruption in the abundant food supply we've grown to enjoy, we need to stock up. For a permanent interruption, as I said before, we'll all (and by all, I mean all the survivors) be eating whatever we grow on our local farms. It takes quite an infrastructure to turn wheat into breakfast cereal, or pigs into bacon, and get it to supermarkets nationwide. It takes electricity and fuel, both of which can be, and has been, in short supply.

You might want to store wheat berries and other grains, then grind (mill) it into flour and bake it into bread and other products as you need it. You'll also need baking soda and yeast and eggs and probably other stuff known only to people who actually know how to bake. I can't, and I know few people who can do more than dump a bag of bread mix and water into an electric bread maker. Also, the storage of wheat and grain in general is actually a potentially dangerous thing if you don't know what you're doing – there are toxic molds that can grow on it if it's not stored properly. It must be pretty dry; you'll need to know how to check the moisture content.

If you decide to store grains (wheat, rye, oats, etc.) you are better off buying it already properly packaged for long term storage by a competent and trustworthy company. Don't get it in hundred pound sacks unless you're feeding a village. You don't want any of your storage products to be in packages larger than you'll use up within a week or two, maybe even a month or more depending of the shelf life after opening and the conditions it's stored under (temperature and humidity). Actually, getting it in sacks won't preserve the product long-term, nor protect it at all from bugs and vermin. Fortunately you can get just about anything in five gallon buckets, packaged in mylar with the oxygen removed. On National Geographic Channels show, Doomsday Preppers, a vendor told of a man who ordered thousands of pounds of wheat for his supply. I can only think that he's planning on reopening the first bakery.

Unless you really know what you're doing when it comes to packaging for long term, staples are best bought professionally packaged. Cooked and freeze-dried (usually in an entrée) is probably the longest shelf life you're going to get. That's also the most expensive way to have these staples.

Fortunately, these days you can find just about anything dehydrated or freeze-dried, and packaged for long term storage. Certainly any fruit or vegetable you can imagine. I've even seen uncooked, freeze dried pork chops – soak in water to reconstitute, and then put them on the grill. I should have bought some while I could, but I will next time I see them.

I'd think everyone has salt and pepper and spices in the cupboard, but if you don't, you should. I'm not much of a cook, but even I have an assortment of spices.

Get plenty of salt, for sure. Iodized would be best if you're not going to have another good source of iodine (and you probably won't). Salt is good for other reasons – gargling with salt water will give you some relief for sore throats if you can't go shopping for over the counter relief at the drug store. If you're going to be cooking great buckets of rice and beans, you need a good amount to salt the boil water. If your salt has an expiration date on it, have a good laugh. Lots of sugar would be handy too, but repackage it in moisture and insect proof jars or Tupperware.

Wheat and Grains

Wheat comes hard and soft, spring and winter, red and white, Durham, and I'm sure I'm leaving some out. Oh yeah, there's Triticale. That's actually real, not just from Star Trek (the original series).

There is all purpose flour, bread flour, whole wheat flour, cake flour, pastry flour, semolina and Durham, self-rising and instant. It can be enriched, bleached, malted, organic, and pre-sifted. There's also buckwheat, and bulgur wheat (for tabouli), and barley and millet and spelt and rye, oh my. The varieties of wheat and their uses are a book in itself. Literally – there are books devoted to the subject! Get one if you're interested. I wouldn't even attempt to explain it all, even if I knew. If you're pretty sure you'll have an oven to bake in, then this is a research project for the specialist. If you can store wheat and grind it, (and whatever other ingredients that are required), all I can say is I wish you lived next door to me.

I understand that there are flat breads that can be made in a frying pan, no oven required. The best I'm going to do is pancakes. I have #10 long-term storage cans of biscuit and pancake mix, and instant oats and other breakfast cereals to be eaten cold or hot, and that will have to do.

Oh, yeah, don't forget that there are people who are sensitive to wheat. They can't eat it. I've read that young children shouldn't have too much of it either. Just saying.

Rice

Most Preppers recommend lots of rice, and I do too. It stores very well, and you only need to simmer it for 20 minutes (see "water"). Not even that long, if it's parboiled (meaning partially pre-cooked and much more expensive). You might appreciate having a stockpile of herbs or bouillon cubes to make it tastier. It is cheap, too. It is a great way to extend freeze-dried meals. Instead of a full serving of the freeze dried meal (which always has a sauce of some sort), you can stretch your good stuff by serving up a filling bowl of rice with a half serving of the main course on top.

Brown Rice is the healthiest, possibly the tastiest, but because it retains its bran, germ, and oils, it is the least shelf-stable type of rice. Unfortunately, kept at room temperature, it can go rancid in a matter of months. It's never recommended for long-term storage, because it just can't be done without freezing.

Enriched White Rice is just white rice, but the manufacturer has replaces some of the vitamin content that was removed when they scrub off the bran and oils. White rice is actually easy enough to store. When I was getting started, I filled a bunch of Mason Jars with Basmati rice ("from the foothills of the Himalayas") and oxygen absorbers. Not much more to it. As it's in glass, I can keep an eye on it for any discoloration. Discoloration means it's oxidizing, or going bad. I would say a mason jar of rice with two jars of water, simmer for 20 minutes, throw in some salt & pepper and a big glop of butter, and/or a bouillon cube, and you have a filling bowl of rice for easily a dozen people.

Converted Rice is a little bit more nutritious than plain white rice, and stores just as well.

Having a large quantity of professionally packaged 5 gallon buckets of rice (and beans) would be an excellent idea, even if you, personally, don't like rice, or beans, or both. At this time, I have two five-gallon buckets of rice, and the beans are on sale this month, so I'm ordering some buckets of them, too. Cost a bit over $1 a pound. As I've said, I don't want to have to shoot my unprepared neighbors to save my food, so I'm planning to feed them instead. I'm not too concerned about them shooting me, not in my neighborhood. Just in case some surprise me and do have guns, as I said, if I let them in on the feeding, they'll be obligated to help defend the food. A large supply of rice and beans that will feed all the neighbors for months will probably be cheaper than inviting them all to a single summer barbecue (if I'm supplying the steaks and beer).

Even if you aren't planning on feeding the neighbors, a couple of buckets of rice and a couple of buckets of beans should not cost much more than about $300 and will provide many hundreds of meals. If you think about it, that, plus a few hundred cans of assorted foods, and you can call it a years' worth of food for under $1,000! It won't be as delicious as my stocks, but it's less than 1/3 the cost.

Beans

Having a variety of buckets of professionally packaged beans, along with rice, is an excellent idea. I would consider pairing them up as essential, as in "essential amino acids". Beans contain all the required amino acids but one, and rice (and other grains) have the missing one. You can actually live on rice and beans even if you never get any more eggs and meat in your life. Consult an educated vegetarian for details!

I regularly cook myself a batch of 13 bean soup, usually with Polish Kielbasa or some other precooked sausage. I always start with a dry mix and soak overnight. I find that when I'm done cooking it after simmering for about 3 hours, there are a lot less beans than I started with, as the faster cooking varieties just disintegrate. It sure tastes good, though. You can feed a lot of people for little money with a big batch of bean soup. Without the meat, to make sure you have complete protein, you need rice (or some other grain). Since I've recently found this out, I've started making batches of rice and beans instead of just bean soup, and it's actually pretty darned tasty. I add some spices, but my first batch was just plain white rice with beans and it was very acceptable.

You can get beans already cooked and canned, but it's much cheaper to get bulk dry beans, and canned beans have a lot of salt added. All dry beans need to be boiled, from as little as 30 minutes to as long as 3 hours. Don't let the pot go dry! Making a batch of rice about 20 minutes before the beans will be ready, as I said, will make a pretty tasty and nutritious meal. Don't forget to add some spices or a bouillon cube in the rice water for added flavor.

With the exception of split pea and lentils (they don't need soaking), you should definitely soak beans overnight, and change the soak water if possible, and definitely give them a good rinse before cooking. This isn't just to reconstitute the beans; it's also a requirement for getting rid of some indigestible compounds in the beans that you don't want to eat. From my research, the optimum soak time is 6 to 12 hours, and that's about right. I always start the soak before I go to sleep, and rinse, drain, and start cooking in the morning.

Dry beans come in many varieties, and the cooking time as well as how much water they absorb varies. The bigger the bean, the longer you should soak them. The longer you soak them, the faster they cook. Soaking begins to dissolve indigestible starches that cause intestinal discomfort. They also expand to 2 to 3 times their size. Beans can be cooked without soaking, but it's not recommended.

I was going to include a guide for how long to cook each bean. Unfortunately, I haven't seen the same answer twice. I've seen people say anywhere from 1 hour to 3 hours for any particular bean. The only good rule of thumb is to cook them slowly – a gentle simmer, rather than a rolling boil. You bring the pot up to a boil and then turn down the heat. Give them a stir and check the water level every 15 minutes or so, and after an hour, you can start checking them for doneness. The beans are done when they can be easily mashed between two fingers (ouch, hot! hot!) or with a fork. I've been doing red, black, and Pinto beans, and about two hours has worked pretty well.

Having a few #10 cans of dehydrated or freeze dried onion flakes available, and whatever else you want to add will make your beans and rice much more delicious. I like adding onions and carrots.

Eggs

I recently ran across an interesting item that you might consider for your food supply. Unless you have a medical problem with eggs, they are an excellent source of protein, and some consider them pretty delicious. The usual powdered egg don't have a great reputation for flavor. They've been around for decades, but no one ever considered them as good as fresh eggs. They're what I consider staples, though.

So far, my stocks contain a fair amount of cans of freeze-dried cooked scrambled eggs. As good as they are, they are pretty pricey too, but I've avoided powdered eggs for this very reason.

There is a company that has developed a new, low temperature process for drying raw eggs that when reconstituted and cooked, are indistinguishable from fresh eggs. I've tried them and it's true. I'll be adding these to my own supply:

http://www.nutriom.com
3145 Hogum Bay Road
Lacey, WA 98516, USA
Phone (360) 413-7269

The product is called OvaEasy egg crystals. It comes in whole egg or just egg whites. They use a low temperature method that results in a better tasting, better quality product that increases the shelf life of dry raw egg from one year to over seven years. From their website:

"Powdered egg shelf-life is only 1 year! OvaEasy· Egg Crystals$_{tm}$ last for 7 years!

Most powdered eggs claim 5 - 10 years shelf-life, but is this really true? Not according to the American Egg Board:

"Plain whole egg solids [powdered egg] have a shelf life of about one month at room temperature and about a year at refrigerated temperatures." www.aeb.org

OvaEasy Egg Crystals have been specially processed using our unique technology to achieve long shelf-life. And since we're a military supplier, we use the US Army Labs shelf-life tests based on the most advanced academic research."

To be totally honest, the paragraph above isn't 100% true, as they aren't taking into account powdered eggs that are specially packaged for long term storage. None the less, the Ova-Easy eggs really are a great product.

They claim their eggs are hormone-free, antibiotics-free, from hens fed a vegetarian diet. The eggs are also pasteurized. You just mix with water and cook like fresh eggs. As of this writing, they'll sell you a single small packet (12 eggs) postage-free so you can try it. There are a few YouTube taste tests that indicate that you can't tell the difference between cooked OvaEasy and fresh eggs, and I can confirm this is true. I'd only add that their measurements (each package has a little measuring spoon) are based on regular eggs. I'm used to using the largest, super jumbo eggs available, so I needed a little more mix than what their measurement considers 3 eggs when I make a 3 egg omelet.

Possibly one of the reasons for their long shelf life claims is that they sell Ova Easy packets in #10 cans.

Butter

I have #10 cans of dried butter powder. You can mix it with water to make a reasonable spread for crackers, bread, etc. Unfortunately, it is not the same as real butter when used for cooking because it contains a lot of milk solids, so it will burn at a lower temperature than real butter. It's not recommended for frying. High temperature will make the fat and water separate, and it'll burn. It can be used for baking, though. Fat chance of that at my house.

If you're going to fry eggs, even reconstituted eggs from crystals or powder, wouldn't it would be nice to have some real butter? Well, that's available for long-term storage too. Shelf life claims vary, but one manufacturer claims a best-by of 8 years, others claim 10 years or more. Either way, canned real butter doesn't need refrigeration until you open it, then it will be just like the butter you're used to. I first found it on

Ready Made Resources: www.readymaderesources.com 800-627-3809 239 Cagle Road, Tellico Plains, TN 3738

They carry 2 brands, Red Feather from New Zealand, and Wijsman & Zonen from Holland. As there are multiple distributors, it might be worth a web search for the best deal.

"There is no Expiration Date written in stone, because the shelf life depends largely on the storage conditions (temperature, humidity, altitude, sunlight/shade, etc.). We do guarantee the shelf life for two years however, the actual shelf life of the butter will

ultimately be determined by the storage conditions (temperature being the main factor) and the seal on the can remaining intact and therefore protecting the butter from the introduction of oxygen. After this, one can expect some nutritional value loss, although it will be edible, provide fat and calories in an emergency, and still be perfectly safe to eat if the can remains sealed."

The makers of Red Feather also have a line of canned cheese you might be interested in.

The University of Utah warns against the home canning of butter. Professionally canned butter might be expensive, at well over $5 a pound, but it's better getting it from a professional company than taking the chance of poisoning yourself.

Milk

If you're planning on breakfast cereal, it either has to be the cans that already have powdered dry milk in it, or you'll need to add milk. As milk is a great source of nutrition, you should have a lot of dried milk on hand. Milk is one of the original "Mormon Four" foods you were supposed to stockpile – wheat, milk, honey, and salt. Of course, this was back in the 1930's, and we've learned a great deal more about food and nutrition since then. Unfortunately, it seems that a lot of people have become lactose intolerant since then, as well. If you are lactose intolerant, you are hereby presented with another special research project – how do you replace the nutrients of milk in your storage? I don't know if there's such a thing as dry soy milk, and as I'm not lactose intolerant, I really haven't done much research about it. I do know the maximum shelf life of soy milk is about a year, so you might be okay. You probably should check out Morning Moo, which is a whey product (more about that later).

Non-fat dry milk, in various forms, is sold by pretty much everyone, and it can be packaged to have a claimed 20 year shelf life, but figure on more like 10, and as I'll explain, maybe you ought to figure on doing some rotating so you replenish your stock every 5 years.

Be aware that some vitamins will decay no matter what the storage conditions are like. I've seen an estimate of 20% a year for A & D, so even though the milk will taste okay and still have useful protein and calcium, after about five years, it will not have any appreciable vitamin A & D left. The problem with drying milk is that is although milk is a good source of vitamins A & D, they are not very shelf stable vitamins; they are sensitive to heat and light. The drying process has destroyed most, if not all of the A & D, as well as other nutrients found in fresh milk. Although the dry milk you buy should have been fortified with A & D (it is added back in after drying), not all dry milk is fortified, and either way you should make sure that you have multiple sources of all the essential vitamins.

The good news is that for almost all humans, regularly spending some time in the sun (with enough skin exposed) will provide enough vitamin D, we were built that way (our skin makes it). For vitamin A, I know liver is a good source – polar explorers have actually poisoned themselves by eating too much Polar Bear liver, as it is too rich in A. If you can't find any polar bears, remember carrots and other vegetables are good sources of carotene which your body converts to vitamin A. If you eat carrots and some other colored vegetables, you'll get beta carotene, and your body converts that to vitamin A, so eat your veggies. Actually, I ready that freeze dried carrots will maintain their beta carotene quite well.

As vitamin A is one of the fat soluble vitamins, you can store up too much (as opposed to vitamin C, which is water soluble – if you have too much, it'll give you diarrhea, but you'll soon flush it all out of your system). In a survival situation, unless you bag a polar bear, your challenge will be getting enough A, not too much. Animal meat, especially organ meats, are the richest sources of vitamin A.

One more tidbit, if you don't have any fats/oils in your diet, you aren't going to be able to even process the fat soluble vitamins, so make sure your storage isn't "fat free". It's easy to get a little fat in your diet every day. Butter is one way, and I'm still working on a bottle of olive oil that must be close to 4 years old and it hasn't gone bad yet, even though it was opened.

I don't know why stores sell fortified and non-fortified dry milk, but you should always choose the most nutrition you can get. By the way, if you see the words "Grade A", that's actually the lower quality stuff. "Extra Grade" is actually a better product than "Grade A".

Whole milk and even low-fat (1% & 2%) milk are very prone to spoilage; the storage life is much shorter than fat free milk, and you probably won't find it from any preparedness store, as it's not suitable for stockpiling. There are dry whole milk products, and they do have shelf lives of over one year, but it's usually only found in the commercial world, for use in bakeries, etc. Even the shelf-stable milks, like Parmalat, are only good for "many months" stored without refrigeration (as with all foods, assume "cool, dry place"). People may not like the taste of the Ultra-High Heat Pasteurized liquid milks, nor fat-free milks, nor dry milks, but you can deal with taste – you still need calcium and protein and the vitamins (the ones added back in) that you get from milk. The taste can be dealt with using vanilla or chocolate flavoring if need be.

There are plenty of choices for instant and non-instant non-fat dry milks available. Get the instant unless you're too poor to afford it – it's much harder to dissolve the non-instant dry milks. There are differences between "dry fat free milk" and "instant dry fat free milk". You probably want to stick to the "instant", unless you have a working blender. The non-instant powder takes up less space, and is usually less expensive, but it is much harder to mix than the instant.

It's better for taste to let the milk sit a little while after reconstituting, rather than using it immediately.

Don't buy dry milk in very large containers, as once opened, they'll spoil (not talking "best-by", talking "toss it") in days, maybe a couple of weeks if you reclose and keep in a cool, dry place. Five gallon buckets are a poor choice for a small family, while a large group might go through more than a bucket a week. Think about that for all your food choices, not just milk.

The only way to make sure you can have all the whole milk you want is to raise cows. Enough said about that.

A preparedness group did a fairly scientific taste test:

www.utahpreppers.com/2010/03/great-powdered-milk-taste-test-and-review/#more-3006

Fortunately for me, the best tasting real (100%) fat-free milk (it actually rated slightly higher than fresh non-fat milk) was the Provident Pantry Instant. As that's the brand I've been buying, it makes me very happy, as I hadn't tried the stuff yet (shame on me). Morning Moo scored higher for taste, but it isn't really milk, it's considered a whey product.

Another product that seems to be popular is **Country Cream brand Nonfat Powdered Milk** www.countrycreammilk.com . The manufacturer is also in business as **Grandma's Country Foods,** http://www.grandmascountryfoods.com **800-216-6466 386 West 9400 South, Sandy, UT 84070**

It's touted as the best tasting powdered milk. Probably, as with OvaEasy, because they use a low-temperature drying method. It's vitamin A & D fortified. They claim a 10-20 year shelf life, which would, of course, depend on storage conditions. You might want to compare the taste with the Provident Pantry brand.

There's another product that seems to be popular with the prepping community. It is

Morning Moo from Augason Farms www.augasonfarms.com **800-878-0099 3431 S. 500 W., Salt Lake City, UT 84115**

"This product is the cornerstone of Augason Farms and responsible for the initial success and birth of the company. Morning Moo's Low Fat Milk Alternative was introduced to the market back in 1972 and has been a huge success ever since. The Morning Moo's product embodies everything that long term storage items should: Extensive shelf life, but still perfect for everyday nutrition and consumption.

Augason Farms is proud to provide a gluten-free version of Morning Moo's, available in both traditional and chocolate flavor. The gluten free alternative still has the same vitamin content as our classic Morning Moo's product. Both contain vitamin D that is vital for the immune system. Deficiency in vitamin D can make an individual susceptible to illness and disease. Our Morning Moo's products also contain Riboflavin. This is a vitamin that is essential for the production of metabolic energy and plays an important role in maintaining healthy skin, eyes, heart and nerves.

Morning Moo's Low Fat Milk Alternative will be very useful in your pantry. It has a huge variety of applications in the kitchen, adding delicious flakiness to pastries, moisture to cakes and working fantastically well with soups, casseroles and a whole host of other delicious recipes."

Morning Moo comes as a dry powder. In a #10 can, the best-by shelf life is, like non-fat dry milk, 20 years if stored properly. As with any other food product, get some so you can try it before you stock up on a lot of it (or, don't do as I do, do as I say).

Don't forget there are also the "non-milk" products like soy milk, and Silk makes a shelf-stable package that should be good for a year, so you'll have to keep it rotating.

Regular non-fat dry milk, whether instant or not, may start losing flavor in just a few years, even packaged and stored properly in #10 cans, and won't last long at all once opened. So, don't load up five gallon pails with the stuff, rotate your stock every few years (what's a few? Open one container after maybe three or four years, if it's fine, try another one in another two or three years. I've got a few cans now, and I'll probably time average a couple or three cans a year. Do what you want with the older stuff I'll probably fertilize the garden with it, I never use non-fat milk myself.

Cooking

If you cook with natural gas from the pipe that runs down your street, it will either work or it won't work. If there's no gas pressure, there's nothing you can do. If you use propane, then you can at least check your storage tank, it's either got gas in it or it's empty. If it's empty, either you can get it refilled or not. If you have an all-electric kitchen, it's pretty obvious you'll need electricity. If the grid fails, you'll need a generator. If you have one, your range, oven, and microwave will work, as long as your generator does. Apartment dwellers probably don't and can't have their own backup generator.

Generators can cost from hundreds of dollars to over $10,000, depending on the size and the fuel. The cheapest ones run on gasoline and are useful for powering some of your appliances but probably not your whole house (certainly not all your major appliances at the same time), and although you may run them continuously, that's only until the fuel runs out or they break. Bigger, much more expensive, self-starting generators may use natural gas or propane, some of the really big units run on diesel (they're like running a stationary truck) and are usually designed to start up whenever the electricity goes off.

Generators use fuel – gasoline, diesel, natural gas, or propane. As long as you have fuel (and don't have a mechanical breakdown), you'll be fine. If you depend on fuel deliveries, you'll have to hope they continue. That's the weak point of your plan. In my area, the power was out for a week in October 2011. Gas stations were closed unless they happened to have a generator to run their pumps, and few of them did. If you had to drive around looking for fuel for your generator, it might have been a long trip.

If you're lucky enough to be set up with solar power, that'll work during the day (some systems even have storage batteries, so you'll have some power at night, too.) They'll work almost indefinitely, as they don't have moving parts (although the cells don't last forever, they'll provide power for decades.)

Generators need maintenance or they'll break down, just like your car. They're really just internal combustion engines that turn a generator rotor instead of a drive shaft. Your car does both. Do you know how to do the required maintenance (which won't matter if you run out of fuel?)

If people hear your generator, they may come to visit, especially people who know you. They'll want to watch your TV, or listen to your radio, or see if your internet works. Are you going to kick them out when it's time for lunch or dinner? What if it's 5 weeks into an event, and they don't have any more food? Are you going to kick them out? "Sorry folks, but it's mealtime, and since we don't want to starve to death like you unprepared losers, we're going to eat. Get lost!" Of course, you might be planning, like I am, to have a lot of extra staples so the neighbors can be fed, for some period of time, anyway. If they have a generator (and you don't), they'll have to let you watch their TV if you feed them.

What if it's not just neighbors, but people with bad intent who are attracted to the sound?

Some people cook with natural gas. Some generators also use natural gas as a fuel. People also heat their homes with natural gas (but need electricity to run the blower if it's an air system, or the pump if it's a circulating hot water system.) As long as the pressure in the system is maintained, you'll at least be able to cook indoors, even if there's no electricity – unless you have a generator too, and we've already looked at that. Even a gas range with electric start (no gas pilot) can be lit with a match and some caution.

Do you have plenty of matches? Back when everyone smoked, everyone had matches. Add plenty of matches to your supply list. I've seen sealed #10 cans of matches for sale at a ridiculous price. You don't need them stored in #10 cans, they're not edible. You can get Diamond kitchen matches, the wood kind that "strike anywhere", for a dollar and change for a box of 300. Order or buy 10 or 20 boxes of them, then package them securely yourself (you're looking for moisture-proof and air tight, but not to the extent that food requires.) I found them at my local supermarket.

Some people cook with propane. Some generators use propane, too. If you use propane, there's going to be a really big propane tank somewhere on the property. Depending on how big it is and how much you use, it could last a long time. If you also heat your house and your water with propane, it'll get used up much faster. If you don't know when your next delivery will be, don't waste it.

Is that big tank of potentially explosive gas you've got bullet proof? If I had (and I have had in the past) a 5 or 6 foot long gas tank in my backyard, I'd think about being prepared to bury it with sandbags or something to protect it if things get really bad. Maybe someone won't look kindly at someone cooking up food that they desperately need themselves, who won't give said food to them, and decide that it would serve you right for being greedy if they were to shoot at your tank with a rifle. That's just something to think about, if things get really bad.

If you happen to be cut off from all outside utilities, and eventually your generator stops due to mechanical failure, or you run out of fuel, how are you going to heat water to cook with, even to just boil water to reconstitute freeze-dried and dehydrated food? There are several alternatives.

My solution is to have a wood burning "rocket stove," and a kerosene stove. Getting a solar oven is on my list, too – it's a no brainer, as they say. I'm not too comfortable storing propane indoors, so aside from the tank for my gas barbecue which is the only use I have for propane now, I'm not going the propane route.

Propane

Propane is very common. If you have a barbecue, there's a very good chance it's either propane or charcoal. Some people have it piped with natural gas. There are also electric ones, but why? Probably for apartment dwellers who can't use flame on the premises, but want to make believe that they are really grilling. Anyway, thanks to barbecuing, most Americans are at least familiar with propane. If you're not, let me remind you – it's a highly flammable, heavier than air gas. You can buy your own containers and have them refilled, or you can get containers that you **swap out empty** for full and not have to refill them (**Blue Rhino** www.bluerhino.com comes to mind). Just about every town has many places to get a tank of propane. I keep a propane tank hooked up to my barbecue grill pretty much all the time, I just shut the valve when not in use, and it seems to last a long time, depending on how much outdoor cooking I do. Some summers I grill daily, some summers less than once a week. There are also smaller containers available to take on camping trips.

Cooking every meal on a barbecue grill is a different story, especially in the situation we're dealing with. You're not going to get a lot of fresh meats and veggies to place on the grill; you're going to be doing most of your cooking in pots and pans.

It wouldn't be very efficient to boil a pot of water on a gas barbecue grill, which is why many grill models have side burners which are designed like your kitchen range – you can put a pot on it and it will use the fuel much more efficiently. You can make do with your grill if it has at least one side burner, but I wouldn't go out and buy a new grill just to have one, unless you have the money to burn. If you are going to buy a new grill anyway, keep that side burner in mind. If you want to do all your survival cooking with propane, then get something built just for it.

Since propane is a popular camping fuel, too, there is no limit to the cooking configurations you can buy. Coleman, for example, makes a wide variety of propane cookers, as well as cookers using their own liquid Coleman fuel, even duel fuel cookers that can use many flammable liquids – they can even use unleaded gasoline, which is a very bad idea except in the most extreme emergency situations.

Any outdoor store will have a big range of propane cooking equipment; you should get the right tool for the job. Cabela's, REI, Bass Pro, and Dick's, and dozens of other stores that deal in camping equipment would be a great place to go see what's available and to compare prices. I've seen tiny little one burners good for boiling a small saucepan of water, to huge outdoor cooking stations that would give any indoor range a run for the money, oven included. That'll come in really handy if you want to bake stuff.

Kerosene

Kerosene is one of the most commonly used cooking fuels in the third world, where people can get a can of kerosene fairly easily, but they usually lack the infrastructure to reliably deliver natural gas and electricity to their homes. Kerosene is a flammable liquid, and is a more refined cousin of diesel fuel. Kerosene is very common, pretty efficient, and fairly safe to store. You'll want to use A1 grade.

As kerosene cookers are very common in India and China, where people don't have much money, kerosene cookers are relatively inexpensive. They are also fairly simple to use – certainly much simpler and less expensive than a US made kerosene heater. I picked up a 22 wick kerosene stove for about $75.

The more wicks, the more heat.

I got mine from

St. Paul Mercantile,
www.stpaulmercantile.com

888-395-1164, 301-616-7549

The wicks are in a circular pattern, held above the kerosene. There are different models with different shapes and number of wicks, and there are also 2 and 3 burner stoves. There's even a small "oven" attachments (about a foot square) that fits over the burner of some stove models. I didn't get the oven, I don't plan on doing much baking, but it's available if you would like to bake, at least small items. Kerosene cookers are pretty frugal with the kerosene, too, but eventually I'll run out of kerosene. Don't forget extra wicks!

A kerosene stove, as with a kerosene heater or lamp, can be used indoors as long as you don't knock the thing over, keep it a few feet away from anything flammable, and you make sure that you have the wick set at the proper height so the flame is blue with little or no yellow (which indicates incomplete combustion, which results in carbon monoxide). When you initially light the device, whichever one you're using, you'll probably get the smell of kerosene for a few minutes. A kerosene flame will also throw a little carbon into the air – meaning that the wall and ceiling closest to it may get a little sooty over time. A small price to pay. It may also be a problem with asthmatics and anyone with a lung condition, so keep that in mind. Even candles put soot into the air. You should also open a window a little for fresh air, as any flame uses oxygen, and enough flames will tend to use up the oxygen in the room. My 22 wick cooker will most likely only get used outdoors, or in the garage with the door open.

The back door, not the overhead door facing the street. No sense in advertising a cookout for passersby.

5 gallon cans of kerosene go for around $25 or so at Home Depot and Tractor Supply (when they have it – it's a seasonal item). I plan to keep adding to my kerosene supply, for cooking as well as heating and lighting. It's a very useful fuel.

If you have the room to store it, you can (maybe) get a 50 gallon drum of the stuff for less money per gallon. I really mean that "maybe" you can. I know they exist, but I've been looking and looking, and although the local heating oil companies will deliver Kerosene, they seem to only do it with tanker trucks, so you have to have your own tank (just like a heating oil tank) for them to deliver into. They aren't allowed to fill a drum, even if I had one. They can only deliver to an "approved" tank. A very expensive (I've been quoted $1,500 for a legally installed 130 gallon, which is the smallest) tank. I'll keep trying to find a 50 gallon drum of kerosene, but it's looking like I'm going to just stock up on 5 gallon cans. I can't justify putting that much money into a tank that I may use someday, especially as I can get about 60 five gallon cans for the money. I'm actually happy enough with the 5 gallon size, even though it's not the most space effective solution.

Rumors have it that kerosene doesn't have a very long shelf life, which is incorrect. Kerosene can last indefinitely if stored properly, meaning not exposed to the atmosphere. A tightly closed metal can or the proper type of plastic container work just fine. There are so many plastics in existence; you have to make sure the one you get is safe for storing hydrocarbons. If you buy it already filled, it's a pretty good bet the supplier used the right stuff, but I wouldn't start filling milk jugs with the stuff without doing some research. Like any other container, don't put it directly on concrete.

The enemy of kerosene is water, and it will absorb water from the atmosphere. There are "treatments" for kerosene available just like dry gas for gasoline, to have on hand just in case, but I don't think it's that important to have them. The reason why is that when I bought my cooker, I also bought a special funnel with it. I needed a funnel anyway, and this one actually filters out any water that may have gotten into the kerosene.

The advertising data on the kerosene cookers I've seen tell you about how much fuel it uses. I think mine is around 8 hours a gallon. Of course I won't be cooking for a straight 8 hours, but I wouldn't be surprised if I burned at least a couple of gallons a week.

Wood

You might be aware of the fact that in some parts of the third world, especially Africa, the people use a lot of wood to cook with, as they really don't have the money to buy any other fuel, and after all, wood grows on trees. Sorry. Because of this, a lot of formerly forested areas are getting denuded. Cooking with wood isn't a very efficient practice, but they do what they've got to do.

In order to conserve wood to slow down the deforestation, as well as try to minimize the lung diseases the locals tend to get breathing in wood smoke all the time, the rocket-stove was invented. The rocket-stove is engineered to burn wood in a way that increases the efficiency, so much so that it burns with a hot, fairly smokeless flame (but it still needs to be used outdoors!) I've got a rocket-stove. That set me back around $100. There's no oven for it, but I did get the water Pasteurizer attachment. There are many dealers and manufacturers of rocket-stoves. The picture makes it look huge, but it's actually only a couple of feet tall, if that. There's a big cook pot on top of it.

I got mine from **Stove-Tec** http://stovetec.net/us

ECOZOOM
Ecological Products for the World

Another supplier   www.ecozoomstove.com

Both suppliers also help out the indigenous people with these things, either supplying them directly, or with the simple manufacturing tools needed to fabricate stoves themselves from locally sourced materials.

In addition to the little personal models, they can also be made out of 50 gallon drums (so that's why I can't find a kerosene drum!). These big stoves are more for village and refugee camp use, although if you've got a big group you're going to survive with, I'm sure you can get a big one yourself.

Solar

The sun is THE source of energy – when it's daytime and not overcast with clouds. Ever used a magnifying glass to start fires, or burn your initials into a park bench? A dark surface in direct sunlight on a summer day really can get hot enough to fry an egg.

Well, there are commercial and do-it-yourself ovens using the same principle of concentrating the sun's rays. There are many different designs, but suffice it to say that just using sunlight, a solar oven can get up to 300 degrees! Granted many baking recipes call for anywhere from 350 to 450 degrees, but I once cooked a turkey in the oven (not in a solar oven) at 275. Of course it took 12 hours, but the idea is that if the temperature is lower, you just cook it longer. It's plenty hot enough to ensure that meats exceed the recommended 160 or so. Where you're going to get the meat is a mystery, but no one is stopping you from using one now. You may even find one big enough to cook a turkey in. It's more like using a slow cooker than an oven. I understand it does a lousy job of browning.

You can pasteurize, and even boil water in them. The boiling water is the part that excites me. Of course, you'll have to be a bit patient, but if it's a clear day, it's a good way to conserve your fuel.

The great thing about solar ovens is that being pretty low tech, basically just reflective surfaces in a framework, they're not that expensive, and I mean that you can make one yourself out of little more than aluminum foil, plastic sheeting, and corrugated cardboard if you've got the plans!

Here's a place to get plans:

www.instructables.com/id/Best-Solar-Oven

For me, I'm going to buy a good sturdy one when I can afford it.

This one is from www.solarovens.org They are a not-for-profit organization that provides solar ovens for the third world. You can get one from them for under $200.

You can make them for free, put them together from inexpensive parts kits, or pay more than $300 for one. Happy shopping.

Charcoal

Charcoal isn't much different from using wood, except it's a more concentrated source of fuel. I'm sure most people are familiar with barbecue charcoal. It comes in "briquettes" as well as odd shaped chunks as that's how it looks in its raw form when it's made. It comes from burning wood without enough oxygen to burn it all the way to ash. The result burns with a nice steady heat without flame – the flames from your barbecue is fueled by the fat from the meat dripping onto them, not the coals themselves.

Charcoal isn't very expensive, but it is rather bulky. It'll have to be stored in a way that humidity won't get to it and degrade it. If you burn it indoors, you will die from carbon monoxide poisoning. If the coals aren't completely out and you throw the ashes away, you're going to start something on fire. Other than that, although I've used charcoal, I don't like waiting for it to be ready so I grill with propane. I don't have any charcoal and I'm not planning to get any charcoal.

Lighting

I'd guess that 99.99% of ordinary lighting in the home is electrical. With the power out, you'll still end up mostly electrical, at least till the batteries run out. There are rechargeable batteries, and there are solar recharging systems available, although they aren't cheap. Those solar charging systems will also charge many cellphones, and even laptops. They're on my list, but pretty close to the bottom.

There are also crank up flashlights as well as crank up radios, and combinations of the two. I've got a couple of cheap crank up flashlights, but there's a secret, you can't just stick them in a drawer and forget them. You have to crank them up a bit every couple of months or so or the device that stores the electricity (the capacitor) will degrade. I do plan on getting the crank up radio, I'd really like to be able to keep up with whatever news is available. More stuff to add to the list, if you'd like.

Next on the lighting list are probably candles. Although they're fairly dangerous, any open flame is. They are cheap, or can be, they can also be expensive if you want the fancy aromatherapy ones. At least with candles, you can throw them in a drawer and forget them till you need them. They're fine for indoors, but it's a risky lighting source if you have to move it around or take it outside. You'd need to put a candle inside a lamp if you want to use it outside, or you'll have to keep relighting it.

If you have a lot of propane, there are propane lamps. If you've got a lot of kerosene, there are kerosene lamps. Add either or both to your list, based on the alternative fuel(s) you decide to go with. Either are designed to be safely used indoors or outdoors (adjusting the flame properly is required). Get extra wicks or mantles, too. Propane lamps would obviously have to be manufactured to greater tolerances than a liquid fueled lamp, but there are kerosene lamps that you pump up so the liquid is pressurized. They're a lot brighter when lit, but also quite a bit more expensive. You can also get really beautiful brass lamps made for indoor decorative use that are gorgeous, and also in the neighborhood of a couple hundred dollars or more. A plain, functional kerosene lamp can be had for $15-20. You decide where your money goes.

Now here comes one you might not have thought of. I didn't till my next door neighbor turned me on to the idea. Ever see those solar powered lights people use to line their driveways? There's a little solar panel on the top, and they charge a battery during daylight and discharge (usually to an LED bulb) when the sun goes down. They come with various powers (milli-amps) of rechargeable battery, and they're good for hundreds of cycles. If the power is out, you should be able to take them into the house instead of leaving them outside. Good idea? I picked up a set of a dozen at Costco that worked out to $5 each ($60 for the set of a dozen). They had cheaper ones at $40 a set. I checked the batteries of both, and in the higher priced set, the batteries were 600 milliamps, the cheaper set was only 400. Proving the more expensive set will either burn longer, be brighter, or some combination.

The ones I have are three part, the stake that goes in the ground, the lamp housing that fits on the stake, and the top part that has the solar charger on top, the batteries inside, and the light bulb at the bottom. That top part is easily removed from the lamp housing with just a twist. You bring that part inside, and put them upside down (bulb side up) wherever you need light. Even if you have no driveway, or even live in a high rise building, you can put just the top part solar-side up on windowsills during the day for charging. Mine have on-off switches, so you don't even have to discharge the batteries if you don't need to, which will extend the life quite a bit. I know there are other nifty solar charged gadgets on the market, I just haven't stumbled across them yet.

For security reasons if you're deep into an event, you will have to determine if it is smart to show any lights from your home at night or not. Lights will definitely attract attention; the question is whether it will be the attention of anyone you really want to notice you. Not everyone is going to be looking to beg food from you or harm you, but it's likely they will be the majority.

If you decide to be blacked out at night, then simply cover the windows from the inside with something to block the light. Go outside at night, and check to make sure whatever you're using really works. I wouldn't paint the windows black or anything drastic like that if you plan on being able to look outside during the daylight. Also, don't forget that at night, if a light is on inside, and it is dark outside, trying to look out the window isn't going to work – but anyone outside will get a great confirmation that there's someone inside. They will be able to see you, while they'll be invisible in the dark. Similarly, during the day, if there is no light on inside, don't stick your face in the window to look out, unless you want whoever may be out there to see you. Stay a couple of paces back from the window. If someone happens to glance by, they're not too likely to see you if you're in the "gloom", but you can see out fine. Of course, if there's a bunch of windows so the inside of the room is bright as outside, then visibility will be the same in both directions.

Heating

If you're in a part of the country that gets cold, well, even Texas will dip below freezing a few times a winter, you are going to want to have a way to heat your home if the event is in the winter. You may have electric baseboard heaters, and those need electricity. You might have central air & heat, and that, too can be all electric. You may have gas heat, but there's an electric blower that distributes the heat through your ducts. Even me, with oil heated circulating hot water need electricity for the pump. Face it, unless you use a wood stove or you've got an old fashioned steam boiler with radiators, you're going to get mighty chilly in a winter with no electricity. I rented an apartment once that had a radiant heater on the wall that used propane. That needs nothing but fuel.

If you're forced to add an alternate method of heating, use some sense and don't try to heat your whole house unless you have to. Maybe the kids will have to double or triple up in a room, instead of all having their own. Maybe the whole family will "camp out" down the basement (if it's finished). You'll figure it out. Whatever you end up using, you won't want to waste fuel if you can help it.

If you can afford it, you can look into getting a wood stove installed. You can buy a wood stove for anywhere from a couple of hundred to thousands of dollars, depends on how big and fancy you want to go. Your local showroom can help you pick the right one for your purposes. Remember, you will also have to have a hole through your wall or roof for the exhaust gas, so you should put a lot of thought into where you'll install it. That smokestack will have to be higher than the highest point on your roof, so that may restrict your installation location. The stack may be able to use your existing fireplace. Check with the experts so you don't void your fire insurance nor burn your house down.

Make sure you keep a good stock of wood, maybe a couple of chords to get you through a winter. You can't have too much wood. A wood stove with proper installation can cost many hundreds of dollars or more, but at least they can usually heat a whole house. Be sure to speak to your insurance agent first, as you'll have to have it properly installed (both inside and out) and inspected or you could void your homeowners' insurance policy. Especially if you want to self-install!

If you have a regular old fireplace, they're well known as an inefficient way to heat – if you don't keep the fire going all the time, the warm air in the room will go up the stack while you wait for the embers to die down and it's cool enough to shut the damper. You can cure that with an insert. They have a door, and are much more efficient. They can be inexpensive, but you also might have to have an insert installed all the way up your chimney, which can get expensive. Get quotes from professionals if you're interested.

There are also wood pellet stoves. I've heard they're great, but all I've got to say about them is that they're great if the pellet factory is still making pellets, and can deliver the pellets to you well into an event, while with a wood stove you can stick any old chunks and lumps of wood into them. I also wonder whether the pellet feed mechanism is electrical? I understand that they at least require electricity for a fan to provide air to the combustion chamber. I could be wrong, but I don't believe you can operate a pellet stove without electricity.

I'm afraid I'm going to have to rely on a kerosene heater. This is a good site to read up on them:
www.endtimesreport.com/kerosene_heaters

 They cost usually between a hundred and two hundred dollars, and are safe for indoor use as long as you follow the directions and keep them several feet away from pretty much anything combustible. They are widely available, Home Depot and other home stores carry them, and there are many on the internet. The only drawback with them is that they pump out a lot of heat, and you can't really dial them down, they're most efficient at close to their maximum. They'll also burn a lot of kerosene, so even turning them on for a few hours, then off, and just cycling them to keep your place reasonably warm can burn up to a gallon a day or more, depending on how warm you want to be and how well insulated you are. I estimate I'll need up to 30 gallons a month, or maybe I can get away with a 5 gallon can a week for however long the winter lasts. Usually, that'll mean I'll need 90 or 100 gallons of kerosene if I want to be cozy. I probably won't use half of that, though. With kerosene currently fluctuating around $5 a gallon, it's not a very expensive way to heat, but you do need to have the kerosene stocked up, and it's much more "hands on" than a thermostat. Heck, you even have to load wood into a woodstove.

People have been safely heating their homes with kerosene for a century. Some people who are off the grill still do.

Alcohol

There's one school of thought that says liquor would be a good thing to stock up on. This obviously isn't a Mormon idea, but the rationale is given as high-proof alcohol is a good antiseptic, it burns clean, and it will always be valuable as trade goods. I can understand that. Stashing a case or two of Scotch, Vodka, Bourbon, whatever, down the basement has its pro's. It also has its con's.

On the one hand, it will never spoil or go bad. Its value for trade will do nothing but increase over time, and with the taxes always going up, it'll never be worth less than what you paid for it, at least the retail replacement cost. A $20 bottle this year could easily be a $50 bottle in 10 years. If an event occurs, sharing a social drink with your group will be relaxing, maybe the only relaxation available.

On the other hand, it all comes in glass containers. Okay, that's a very minor negative. Keep it in a case and it's probably going to be fine. Also, you really need to make sure this particular stash stays secure.

If people know you are stashing freeze dried food and beans and rice in your basement, who would really care? Unfortunately, if the neighborhood teens find out you've got a lot of booze in your basement, it could be just the prize needed to encourage them to commit burglary someday. How about your own kids? Is the booze stash going to be secure enough from them and their friends? Just something to think about.

During an "event", people will be stressed, some people extremely so, but not the "had a hard day at work!" stress. More like "is life as we know it over, and will we survive this?" level of stress. Perhaps that is too much stress for alcohol to handle. If things have gotten bad, and people take to being armed all the time, well, if you don't know by now that alcohol and guns don't mix, maybe you should have neither.

The last people I'd want to be around are drunk, stressed out people whose lives have completely changed for the worse. Even if I was the only one with a gun, and I wasn't drinking, do you think having a gun matters to a drunk who decides to get into a fight with you, for any reason or no reason at all? Being three times their size and an expert in martial arts doesn't matter to a drunk. I can assure you that nothing matters to a drunk, because a part of the brain of a drunk is away on a holiday, and unfortunately it's the part you really need to have available to make rational decisions with. That's why drunks regularly jump into cars and kill people, among a whole lot of other really stupid things. Believe me, in my time as a police officer, I've seen a lot, and in most situations that have gone bad, as the saying goes, "alcohol was a factor".

So think long and hard about whether alcohol will be a part of your survival supplies, and if so, how much and for what purposes. If you need an antiseptic, you can store denatured or isopropyl alcohol. Perhaps a couple of bottles for medicinal use is reasonable, as alcohol does make for a workable anesthetic if there's nothing else to use, and you need to give someone stitches or reset a joint.

Getting down to the truth, though, your decision, probably, is really whether you want to be able to get a buzz on or not. The deciding factor is whether it can really be limited to just an occasional buzz, or will it lead to an unfortunate incident at some time in the future when you can least afford to have unfortunate incidents? Think hard about this in advance, because I'd bet money that in case of an "event", the first place to be looted are the liquor stores, so there will be no second chances to get alcohol. I just hope anyone who decides to come and take my supplies are pretty liquored up – talk about an easy target!

First Aid & Medical

You may not be a paramedic, but I'm sure most adults in America have the knowledge to at least treat a cut or abrasion. If not, let me remind you – clean the wound, stop the bleeding with direct or indirect pressure, use something that will prevent infection, and use and change clean bandages as needed. You'll at least need a basic first aid kit. They do get fairly expensive, but better to have more than you need than less. You'll never know if when you need it, perhaps someone who will really know what to do with it will be available. It would be better to have more first aid supplies than you know what to do with, than to end up wishing you had something you don't.

If you're part of a group, or just a family unit, maybe one of you might volunteer to read a first aid book, and be the group "medic". If you can't call the police, you probably won't have much luck with an ambulance, either. The reality is that everyone who takes care of the general public will most likely have people of their own to take care of. If the situation is bad enough, any public servants still on the job will have their hands full.

As with supermarkets awaiting a resupply that may not come for a long time, pharmacies are in the same boat. I realize that there are rules, but if you are dependent on any medication, you should try to somehow, through hook or crook, amass yourself as much of a stockpile as you can, keeping the shelf life in mind. This could be one of the situations that being open about prepping can be a good thing.

Perhaps your doctor is willing to humor you, and if your medication isn't on a controlled substance list, the doctor may be able to help you out mentally by providing the means for you to get an extra two or three month supply to calm your fears. Let the doctor know why you want the extra supply, and be sure to turn in any of the meds as they expire so he knows that you're really just maintaining the supply for emergencies and you're not reselling it or doing anything else with it on the side.

It's got to be worth a try, because it you're going to stockpile food for when it isn't available, it only makes sense that you should stockpile medicine that isn't going to be available either.

In case you weren't aware, unlike food in cans that are edible long after their nutritional value plummets, medicines aren't necessarily like that. If you take a certain dosage, and the stuff degrades over time, your dosage isn't going to do the same thing as if it was fresh.

Some medicines and I think I've read that even aspirin and some antibiotics, can degrade and actually become toxic when it gets too old. So make sure you ask your doctor to get you up to speed on what the real shelf life is for your medicines (your pharmacist is probably more expert, but they can't GIVE you any meds, only the doctor can), and whether you'll need to take more of the old stuff to be effective or throw it away because it goes bad.

If you need medicines like insulin that need to be kept refrigerated and have a seriously short shelf life, I don't know what to tell you. You'll need to have a serious conversation with your doctor about it, and just hope that you're prepared for the longest term event that is reasonably possible for you.

You can figure that many drugs are labeled to expire two years from manufacture, but they can still be effective for a few years after that. Some drugs were tested by the military and found to be good up to 15 years from manufacture! Be careful though, other drugs may have degraded so much that they're literally poison.

www.terrierman.com/antibiotics-WSJ.htm

If you are on a medication, you need to research what the REAL expiration date is, so you'll know how much you can stockpile and how long it'll last. Then you have to get your doctor to provide you with as much of a supply as is reasonable.

If the power is out, I doubt if doctors are going to be keeping office hours. They're likely to be home trying to survive with their families. At least medicine isn't going to devolve back to bleeding out the bad humors, but hopefully (in my temporary "event" scenario) things will get back to normal before too many of us succumb to preventable or treatable illnesses. I don't know what else to say about the subject.

If you have to suddenly switch from your normal food to your survival food, there is the possibility that there can be some, let's say gastro-intestinal consequences to this change. Until your body starts getting used to the changeover, you can experience anything from diarrhea to constipation. It would be a good idea to have some over the counter remedies to ease the symptoms of these discomforts. I haven't seen anything about this in my research, but the longer shelf life items would be dry powders and tablets like Metamucil for constipation, and Imodium for diarrhea. If symptoms last for more than two or three days, it could be something more serious, and in that case, it's beyond my knowledge to tell you what to do.

Diarrhea can be from an infection, which could be a virus, bacteria, irritable bowel syndrome, lactose intolerance, gluten intolerance, and many more. If it's bacterial, then the diarrhea is good, it will flush your system and you don't want to stop it. Imodium (loperamide) works by slowing down peristalsis, and Pepto-Bismol (bismuth subsalicylate) works by changing the fluid balance in the intestines. Taking anti-diarrheals for too long can also (rarely) cause medical problems of their own. See the following articles for more info: www.mayoclinic.com/health/diarrhea/DS00292/DSECTION=treatm ents-and-drugs

www.drugs.com/condition/diarrhea

Over the counter medications for constipation (Laxatives) are generally fiber. Eating beans and rice should give you plenty of fiber. MRE's will not give you enough fiber. Metamucil, Citrusel, and Benefiber are very safe to use, short term. Medications like Ex-Lax are harsher. See □

www.mayoclinic.com/health/laxatives/HQ00088
www.drugs.com/drug-class/laxatives

If you can score a supply of antibiotics, I doubt if they'll go to waste!

Hygiene

Oral

As I'm personally sporting lots of fillings and a few gold crowns in my mouth, and financed great vacations for several dentists, I can tell you that oral hygiene is high on my list. I use an electric ultrasonic toothbrush now. Wish I did when I was a kid. It won't work after the rechargeable battery fades if I can't plug in the charger.

I also have a couple of dozen manual toothbrushes I've accumulated over the years. I get a freebie every time I go to the dentist, and I've picked up a couple of warehouse store sized packages over the years. They never go bad, although they will wear out. So, have a handful of toothbrushes available for each member of the family, and don't forget the floss.

I've got no idea what the shelf life is of a tube of toothpaste, I'm sure it's at least a few years, but a supply of that would be wise. Get a good amount of the toothpaste of your choice, and fluoride would be smart – you don't drink it, it's just applied to the teeth, so if you're one of those anti-fluoride in the drinking water people, chill out - there's nothing wrong with a topical application!

I also highly recommend those soft wooden "interdental stimulators", kind of like a book of matches that contains toothpicks that you break off as you use them. They're great for cleaning between teeth. They're softer than toothpicks and they're shaped perfectly.

If you don't get cavities, you won't miss not having dentists around. A long event will be bad news if you do get a cavity, or impacted wisdom teeth, or abscesses, or need a root canal. Prevention is job #1.

You might as well also pick up stuff like clove oil and any other likely looking over the counter mouth related remedies and add them to the first aid kit. It might take a while to get a dental appointment during an event, so you should be ready for pretty much anything that you can do help yourself. I don't expect anyone to be doing cavity filling as a home remedy, but you can at least try to do something about the pain in case something does go wrong in the dental area.

Bathing

Depending on your setup, taking long hot showers may have to be put on hold for a while. That doesn't mean you can't clean yourself, but it does mean you may be standing in the tub with a bucket of water and a washcloth. There are lots of "cleaning towels" in packets advertised on survival sites, but that's going to run up your bill, they're more for the bug-out bags. What's wrong with the terrycloth items you already have? It'll just mean a little extra laundry to wash.

 There's a camping shower, available from most preparedness stores, which is basically a bag you fill with water (a good 30 pounds of water), hang it from someplace that is both sturdy and somewhat taller than you are, that has a hose and shower head coming out the bottom. You stand under it, and let it flow. Don't put it in your living room unless it's equipped with a floor drain. Pictured is the Stearns Outdoor Shower available from Cabelas for around $20-30. It's basically just a bag you fill with water and hang. If you hang it in the sun for a while, you can even have a warm to hot shower. There are many more portable devices, that go all the way up to completely self-enclosed units if you want to spend the money on one. If you've got things set up with a manual well pump, as I said, it can be plumbed to the house pipes, and you can then take a shower while someone is out there pumping. It'll be cold, though. I think a bucket of warm water and a washcloth may be more comfortable.

Just in case you never thought about it, short hair is much easier to take care of than long hair. It needs a lot less shampoo, too. Plus, there are items you probably never thought to stock up on, like lice medicine, so having a good pair of scissors just in case you decide that going short is a good idea. Clippers would be great if there was power, but we had scissors long before we had electricity.

I saw a guy the other day on YouTube. He was pretty proud of himself; he learned how to make his own soap – lye soap. I've got a better idea. For $30, maybe $50, I can go to the warehouse store and buy a lifetime supply of Irish Spring or Dove or whatever else they have. If the event is TEOTWAWKI, I'll let the next generation worry about making and using lye soap!

Laundry

Doing the laundry will most likely devolve into agitating your clothes

in a big bucket, so make sure you have a big bucket. Maybe have two big buckets, one for the soap, one for the rinse. A good supply of laundry detergent wouldn't be a bad idea either. Smacking your clothes on a rock at the riverbank used to be the way to go, but somehow that leaves me with an itchy feeling all over. There are actually manually cranked clothes washing machines available. The one above is around $50, available from www.cleanairgardening.com as well as other places. They don't appear to be able to do very large loads, but you may have plenty of extra time on your hands.

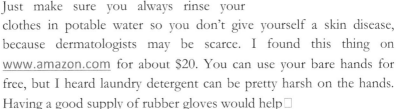

There's also what are basically sticks with a wide ring arrangement on the end to be used to agitate clothes in that big bucket. Just make sure you always rinse your clothes in potable water so you don't give yourself a skin disease, because dermatologists may be scarce. I found this thing on www.amazon.com for about $20. You can use your bare hands for free, but I heard laundry detergent can be pretty harsh on the hands. Having a good supply of rubber gloves would help □

I've talked about doing the laundry, so I need to mention clotheslines. What's that? If you're under 30 or so, I understand your confusion. Maybe you've seen it on TV or in a movie. Once upon a time, after you washed your clothes, instead of throwing them in a box and pressing a button, you had to throw them over a rope that was tied between two fixed objects, such that the wind and sunlight (natural evaporation) will dry them. You

did this because wet clothing tends to get moldy if put away into warm dark places like drawers and closets. So make sure you have two such fixed points in mind, and enough rope to reach between them – but not too much rope, if they drag on the ground, what's the sense of washing them? There are also these devices called clothes-pins you use to hold the clothes onto the rope, else a gust of wind may send your laundry flying all over the neighborhood. They might be old-fashioned, but they're still widely available.

You can also hang your clothes up indoors; there are many foldable gadgets that are made for the task. They work okay in the winter when the humidity is low, but it could make things uncomfortably humid in the summer. Google "clothes

drying racks". You can also put them outside, but as is apparent, a good wind will knock them down. They at least give you a chance to dry your clothes if you don't have a clothesline, or it's raining. They also can be had pretty cheap. I've seen people put clothes out on lines in the winter. Clothes can actually be freeze-dried!

Toilets

You may find that your current facilities work just fine no matter what happens. With well water and a septic system, you may find this small but essential part of life relatively unaffected. You may have to use a bucket of water to flush with, but there's nothing like the continuity of using your own throne.

Some of us are not so fortunate. We may need alternate accommodations. The first option that comes to mind is to continue to use the toilet in the home, but if the plumbing isn't working, what you do is first drain all the water out of the toilet – tank too, so nothing starts growing in there. Then you line the inside of the toilet bowl securely with plastic – tough stuff, not food wrap! Duct tape it in place. Then, you must have a good supply of plastic trash bags, kitchen sized is fine. The cheaper the better. You put that bag into the bowl, making sure that is secure, use the toilet, and when you're done, you can get rid of the bag. Tie a knot in the bag as low as you can so you can snip off the excess, so you minimize the amount of plastic – more on that later. You will need hundreds of bags, maybe more, so start collecting. I alone would want at least 365 a year, a family of four, well you do the math. Can you double up, or more? That's up to you guys. I'll bet the closer you get to running out of bags, the more aroma you will put up with to save bags.

What to do with the bags? Well, that is a problem. Depends a lot on where you live, the lay of the land, the closeness of your neighbors, and other factors.

You could build an outhouse. That will take a very big hole, and in the summer with no one to come pump it out, a lot of fortitude, and in the winter, a wooden seat for sure! If this is something possible for you, that's a homework assignment. I'm sure there are plans on the internet. Hey, this is doable – what do you think people did before there was indoor plumbing?

So back to the bags. You will soon understand why plumbing was used back in Roman times, by the rich anyway, and possibly earlier. Ideally, you're going to need a very big, very deep hole in the backyard, far from the house and far from a well if you have one. When I say deep, I don't mean a couple of feet, that'll fill up pretty fast and anyway, when the hole is full, you'll need room to put at a couple of feet of dirt on top of it. Maybe you could also throw a thin layer of dirt in there from time to time? You'll want to separate the flies from the poo, as much as possible. In the winter, it won't be so bad (if you're up north) but in the summer, I'll leave it to your imagination. Those bags will probably percolate and burst. Don't give this short shrift – this is a major potential disease maker, flies will make sure they pass around whatever microorganisms that percolate out of your cesspit. Professionals would keep a big bag of lye around, to occasionally throw a layer on top. If no lye, soil will have to do. Guess where any disposable baby diapers have to go?

As long as I'm letting my imagination run with this, I'd say that if it's truly a bad event, then I doubt if the fire department is going to come by and give you a citation if you occasionally pour some flammable liquid into your cesspit and light it. I once saw in a Viet Nam War movie, that under the outhouses were 50 gallon drums, and a detail would regularly have to pull out the drums and burn them with I guess it was gasoline or diesel fuel. Can't see why something like that wouldn't work here. I would be aware of which way the wind is blowing for this kind of an activity. Aside from anything else, just the burning plastic will give off dense black toxic smoke! The neighbor downwind may decide you're using chemical weapons against him, and may retaliate!

I picked up a portable toilet at Cabelas that also uses bags. The bags they sell are extremely expensive, we're talking over a couple of dollars a bag, because they have chemicals in there that sanitize and deodorize. They're great for camping out on for a weekend, and I suppose if you need them for the first week or two, they'll solve the problem, but for possibly months? That'll sure add up! I want to invest my money in the food, not on the other end of the process.

Etcetera

Since bathing is going to be such a pain, we may end up back to the days when you only did it once a week. In the meantime, people are going to get smelly. Don't forget to have a good supply of deodorant. I've heard that those deodorant "rocks" actually do work, and last a long time. I haven't tried it personally, but people who have used them say they work, but only as a deodorant, not as an antiperspirant.

With no scientific testing, I would hazard a guess and say that the shelf life on a solid stick type deodorant is longer than the alcohol-gel type, only because solids last longer than liquids over time. This is definitely one of those "choose what you like" situations. The big outlet stores like Sams Club and Costco usually sell this stuff in those big "lifetime supply" packs. Get a few!

Being a man, I am only vaguely aware that women have their own specific hygiene needs. I will just bring up the point that if you are a woman, you should figure out what and how much you will need and get those supplies stocked away, especially anything that you can't live without.

As you do more research, you're going to find that a lot of people painstakingly produced lists of things you should have. You may find you've already got a lot of what's on those lists, but you may see things that neither you nor I have thought of. Rolls of duct tape, tools to cut down trees, all sorts of things. It would be worth your while to look over those lists for more good ideas.

Clothing

During an event, business suits and slinky cocktail party dresses will most likely go out of fashion, or at least be on hold for the duration. Not only may dry cleaning become a fond memory, but as I've mentioned, laundry will most likely be done by hand in big buckets, in small batches. Wash and Wear will be all the rage.

You can pretty much expect that every day will be the weekend, so if you consider your wardrobe, and you find it very heavily weighted towards looking good as opposed to being sturdy and comfortable, especially footwear, you have a bit of shopping to do. With no idea how long the situation will last, you should have comfortable shoes with a spare or two for good weather, and the same for bad weather. Jeans, painters pants, and cargo pants will be all the rage, and don't forget the rugged winter wear.

Natural fibers, I've heard, are the best for the hard-working Prepper. Camouflage patterns may save you someday if you're being chased by any bad guys, but that's if there's some woods to hide in, cammo doesn't work as well for paved streets and sidewalk environments, but there's no reason you can't go cammo. Any dark clothing is good, it won't show dirt as much, and won't show you as much if there's a need to be on security patrol. Of course, light colors would be nice to have, especially shirts, for the summer season.

If the event is very long-term, it might be a while before your next shopping trip, or even the next boatload of clothes showing up from China and making its way to your local shopping center or mall.

I know that an excuse for stocking up on clothes may get some of you very excited, but you probably don't want to stockpile more clothes than food, so keep your budget appropriately balanced. Going out to get 10 more pairs of designer jeans isn't worth it if you starve before wearing out two or three pairs of them. More food – less clothes!

It's been said of some children that they grow like weeds. I had a friend in junior high school that went away for a summer and I'd  swear he came back six inches taller! If you've got some fast growing children or adolescents, you're going to have to really exercise your brain cells to figure out what to do about dressing them. I don't have children, so you'll be the experts on this one.

Once you outgrow a pair of shoes, there's no going back to them. That's no joke. As a men's size 14 myself, it's hard enough to find the right shoes in normal times. You might get away with going barefoot in the summer, but what about winter? You going to wrap your kids feet in rags like they had to do during the revolutionary war after their boots wore out? Don't forget, the odds are that you're not going to be dragging that accident-prone rug rat of yours to the emergency room like you can now, so you must protect their feet. A bad cut on the foot during an event can mean being crippled, if not dead from infection! Places like Walmart usually carry what I used to call chukka-boots, quite sturdy, and inexpensive. You might be able to "bracket" those feet of the future by getting the next couple of sizes up when you next go shoe shopping. As their feet grow, you already have the next size up, and keep going like that as time goes by. If your kids feet are like mine, you'll never stop this process. These don't look too cute for girls, but in an extended event, cute and stylish is the last thing anyone should worry about.

Buying and storing a lot of clothes that exactly fit a 12 year old now may mean a lot of rags if they aren't needed for 2 or 3 or 5 years. Maybe there's a younger sibling who will finally fit in them by then. Whatever you decide to do about clothes for your kids, one thing I will tell you is that style should be of absolutely no concern. They're going to wear whatever fits and be happy about it. So plan to decorate your kids the way you would your home if you were selling - lots of earth tones, nothing loud or obnoxious. Also go for sturdy and long wearing.

Oh yeah, I know men don't have to worry about this as much a women do because most mens pants need belts, but I've seen a lot of womens slacks that don't. Make sure that you have belt loops in all your pants, as most of us will be losing some weight (potato chips and ice cream having such short shelf lives). If it isn't going to suck so badly, I'd almost be looking forward to an event so I can get back to my fighting weight!

If anything good comes out of an event, obesity will be on the decline. So don't ever toss out old clothes just because you don't fit in them anymore. Get some of those plastic vacuum storage bags and you can store a lot of old clothes in a small space, for a time when you can fit into them again. Actually, I've had my clothes storage preps done for a long, long time, because I hate to throw away perfectly good clothes just because I can't fit into them anymore, and I've ratcheted up the waistline a few times over the years.

As far as those CBN (Chemical, Biological, Nuclear) full body suits go, sure, if you want to spend money on them, go ahead and eliminate a source of anxiety for yourself. For me, if things are so bad we've got to hermetically seal ourselves to protect us from germ warfare or fallout, it's probably one of those "the living envy the dead" situations, and I've already given you my philosophy on that.

Babies

Women have been having babies throughout history, under every conceivable circumstance. Wars, famines, you name it, the consequences of an evening nine months earlier show up no matter what the world decides to be like at the time. I'm not speaking as a parent, only an innocent bystander, but I know that there is a large pile of supplies needed for babies. They go through a lot of food, and a lot of diapers.

I would think that jarred baby food will have a similar shelf to cans. I would also think that canned baby formula would have a good shelf life as well. Are you going to fill a room with two years' worth of cases of Enfamil or Similac or something like it? Something for you to look into.

If you already have a baby, you know much more than I do about it, and if you have a baby on the way, I'm sure that this has become a major research project for you. If not, get the heck on the ball! The kid's not going to take care of itself for a couple of decades, at least - you know?

I can see people storing tons of powdered formula and disposable diapers, and let's hope they never need to use them, but they're certainly items that you'll have no problem rotating at all. If you have a baby, or have one on the way, you will have to add those specific baby items to your supplies and maybe you'll be able to pass them on to someone else and never need to use them yourself, but if you do need them, you're going to be very happy to have them, won't you?

As far as the actual birth, about all I know about that is the training I'd received in the police academy, and what I remember most about it is that I never wanted anyone giving birth inside MY cruiser! If there is a baby on the way, just remember that women have been giving birth long before anyone thought to invent obstetricians and hospital delivery rooms. It should be okay! Midwives did the trick for centuries, and there may even be a registered midwife in your area – good to know just in case, you know?

Finances

Many Preppers recommend having a good amount of cash available, and I mean in your possession, not in an ATM machine. You might as well, it's not like you'd be missing out on any interest if you leave it all in the bank. If there's no power, the ATMs won't work, the banks won't be open, and it's possible that the bank employees will be a little too busy trying to survive to take the time to go to work so you can get cash. Cash will most likely work just fine for the duration of an event, if it's going to be of a reasonable duration and people know it. You'll be hard pressed to find anyone too interested in money, if the situation is such that food is in short supply.

If the event is caused by a financial collapse, well, if you run cash through the wash a few times it'll make dandy toilet paper. If it's just lights out, cash will be the only way to buy things, if there's anything for sale, and if there is, prices won't be cheap. The FEMA trucks, if they show up, won't be charging for whatever rations they will be giving out. Whatever you get, your tax dollars already paid for.

Credit cards either need electricity to run them, or a vendor will have to trust you and do it the old fashioned way by running an impression of the card, or just writing the information on paper and sending it to the card company whenever it's again possible to do so. Again, that's if there are any vendors in business at the time.

I've read a lot of discussions about getting out of debt, which is always a good idea, but in the event of a major, long term event, I doubt if the bank is going to come try to foreclose on your house. Everyone will be in the same boat, and if things get back to normal, there will be time enough to straighten things out. There's no sense in getting into too much detail about this, as no one could possibly know what is in the future. That old crystal ball conundrum again.

If you've been accumulating gold and silver, that's a good thing. Hopefully, you've made a bundle, at least on paper. Ever think about what happens if things get *really* bad? Can you eat that metal? Do you think someone who has food, and you don't, will trade you food for gold? Maybe, but keep in mind, they can't eat gold either. If things get back to normal in just a few months, your precious metals may retain a lot of value, but if the economy collapses, and people don't have money, then there will probably be little demand and the value of your precious metals will collapse too! Remember, food will never cost less than it does now, so pre-buying food will protect your investment just like having precious metals will, and although metals go up as well as down, the value of food will never go down. An advertisement says "Gold has never been worth zero" – well, neither has food!

I have some precious metals, and I sold some recently to get a couple of good rifles and ammunition. You might consider cashing in some of your metals to give your food storage a kick start, or get some protection, if you need to.

Sure, if nothing happens, you'll be sad to have sold a couple of ounces of gold for $3000 when someday it might double in value, but on the other hand, if you try to get desperately needed food, that same gold might only be worth a couple of weeks' worth of rations, if anyone wants your gold at all – they won't know if things will get back to normal, so whoever trades you precious food for precious metal will be taking quite a chance. Those same two ounces of gold will get you a years' worth of really good food right now.

Security and Defense

The power was out in my area of New England for around a week in October 2012. There was no looting. There were no gangs of hungry zombies looking for food. No one starved to death. If there were burglaries, they didn't even make the news (of course, there was no access to news, except for battery powered radio, until the power came back on). Some people went to work; some people didn't if there was no power at their workplace. Defense requirements – no more than at any other time. Lock your doors, close and lock your windows, situation almost normal.

Even in normal times, burglaries happen all the time. It is far rarer for people to have their home invaded by armed criminals, but it does happen. If the blackout lasted two weeks, the situation would probably be the same, maybe less as most people will be home all day. What happens if something much more serious happened? As the weeks go by, if things don't get back to normal, more and more people will become increasingly desperate. As I discussed earlier, there's no reason to think that an "event" must happen in our lifetime. I hope nothing ever happens. I look forward to having a very low food budget in retirement, as I'll be eating food I've already paid for.

As with having food as insurance, one must also have security insurance. As the saying goes, when seconds count, the police will be there in minutes. Even in normal times, I'm almost certain there isn't a police officer posted outside your door. Every year, there are countless instances of attempted as well as successful break-ins. The police may get there while the perpetrators are still there, if someone manages to notice and call the police in time, and the police response time is quick enough. Most often, and I speak from personal experience, the police show up to take reports about the crime, they almost never prevent it, and rarely catch the perpetrators in the act. If you aren't capable of defending yourself and your loved ones, you might end up as one more sad statistic.

Legal and Moral Aspects of Self Defense

Fortunately, as an American Citizen (with no criminal history, etc.) you have the right to be armed, in the home if not out in public. Being armed is a right, but it comes with an awesome responsibility. Training in the laws, in gun safety, in gun handling and use, are just the prerequisites. The ability to easily take the life of another person is not to be taken lightly. The foolish storage of guns where children can get at them may inadvertently make you a child murderer. On the other hand, being totally defenseless, having to rely on the police to come and take a report is also, in my opinion, pretty foolish as well.

I'm not going to speak about gun laws other than explain that they differ from state to state, as well as city to city. If you decide that you are going to be armed, it is your responsibility to comply with the applicable laws, and get training even if there is no requirement to do so where you live. If you buy a gun and don't know how to handle it and use it properly, you're a danger to yourself and others, and probably not so much to an assailant.

The most important thing to learn is not when you **CAN** shoot, but rather when you **MUST** shoot. "Can" means you had the choice not to. "Must" means you had no choice at all.

Choosing to shoot when you could have reasonably avoided it is a good way to end up in jail. Using a firearm at all will in most jurisdictions almost certainly result in your arrest. If you actually hit someone, the "almost" part of my last statement goes away.

If you ever find it necessary to shoot an intruder, it will be in your best interest, at this time, to be far too upset to give any statement to the police. Am I giving you legal advice? No, I am giving you Constitutional advice. I have nothing against the police, as I was the police, and after everything I have seen and heard, I know this to be true - anything you say may be held against you in a court of law. That isn't just for TV. ANYTHING you say, so say nothing at all. The police will not necessarily be happy that you are slowing down (not hindering!) their investigation, but tough.

They presumably have a shooting victim, they also should have a discharged firearm as well as the shooter – you. The incident is over, no one else is at risk, there's no reason to rush anything at this point forward. Anything else they need to know, they can be patient and wait for your lawyer. Most people are their own worst enemy; they may say really stupid things that get them into all kinds of trouble. Follow that old adage about how you may be thought a fool, but don't open your mouth and remove all doubt.

Whether you are arrested or in the rare case you are not arrested, anything you say may later be interpreted or mis-interpreted by a jury or enthusiastically anti-gun District Attorney to show that you are a danger to society, no matter how deserving of being shot your poor unfortunate "victim" was. You will need a lawyer at this time more than you probably ever thought you would, but you do. Always keep in mind, you may think that you are 100% in the right, but what you think has nothing to do with it, so zip it! Or as they say, they'll give you enough rope to hang yourself. You certainly should be too upset to think straight, much less have rational a discussion after just being involved in a shooting! Or do you shoot people all the time? No? Have you ever thought about it? Have you ever thought about what you would do in this situation? Were you confident that you could actually shoot someone? How did you know that you wouldn't hesitate, or freeze up? Keep talking, keep digging a hole for yourself. Eventually you'll look like a premeditated murderer, all you needed was a victim to present himself to you so you could get your thrill of the kill, just like you always wanted to, like you've been hoping you could? See where I'm going with this?

Discuss the details privately with your attorney, who will be representing you and trying to keep you out of prison. You cannot assume that anyone else involved will be on your side, even if they tell you they are. No one else really is there to help you. They are there to determine as many facts about the situation as they can. Your state of mind is very relevant. Whatever you say will be recorded, even if "that didn't come out the way I meant it". You cannot be in any more trouble for NOT talking to the police, especially if they have decided to arrest you. Even if they don't initially arrest you, they can talk to you for hours, and something you say may convince them that they must arrest you.

DO NOT make the mistake of thinking or being convinced that having legal representation means you feel or are guilty about anything. You can apologize to the officers for holding up their investigation all you want, but you aren't required to make any statements, so don't. Name, rank, and serial number, sorry, I need a lawyer, I can't answer any more questions. That's it.

If you shoot someone, and the circumstances truly do not matter, you are in a serious situation that will possibly have repercussions that can last for the rest of your life. There is almost no statement that you can make that will eliminate that near certainty of arrest, but you might make a statement out of ignorance or sheer stupidity that will almost guarantee a conviction.

The responding Law Enforcement Officers are most likely not going to make a determination of whether a shooting is justified on the spot. The entire scene will be examined by specially training investigators, and there may be forensic testing required as well. If you are allowed your freedom during this time period, it would only be because you have a squeaky clean background and the facts of the situation so far are such that they are willing to give you the benefit of the doubt. GET A LAWYER! They can always come back and arrest you later. The file will go to the District Attorney, or County Prosecutor, or whatever they have in your jurisdiction. They will have their own personal bias about guns, and civilians having guns, and especially civilians using guns on other civilians. They need to have the specific facts of the incident. Then, they will determine if those facts fit THEIR interpretation of the written laws regarding legally justified self-defense, and will decide to go to trial if the facts don't seem to fit. Motivation matters. Give them your personal philosophy and like I say, a bunch of rope, they may just decide to hang you if they can get away with it.

Just one more thing I want to mention. The odds are high that if you are involved in a shooting incident, you will be tested for drugs or alcohol. Being under the influence of anything will compromise the perception that your decision making process was not impaired. What I mean by this is that the prosecutor or even the jury may assume that if you were "in your right mind", you may not have had to shoot. Back to that "guns and alcohol don't mix" truism. Just something you should know.

Practical Aspects of Defense

So, to repeat, choosing to shoot when you could have reasonably avoided it is a good way to end up in jail. Unfortunately, the definition of "reasonable", of course, is not up to you – it's up to the District Attorney or Prosecutor, or it may be up to the jury of your peers, at your trial. So let's be more practical. I'm going to assume you have a firearm. If you don't, you may be the knucklehead who brings a knife or a baseball bat to a gunfight. We are talking about getting yourself armed for self-defense, in case you find yourself in a situation where calling the police just doesn't work anymore.

The common guideline in the United States is that you can use deadly force to protect yourself or another person from imminent (legalese for immediate) death or severe injury. Severe injury meaning it may result in death. Fistfights rarely result in severe injury or death. A beating with a baseball bat or tire iron may, but not necessarily must meet the requirement. A knife, sure, that's a deadly weapon, but was he 10 feet away, or 50 feet away? Guess what? If he was 3 feet away, he will probably stab you before you could draw and fire a gun. It he's 50 feet away, who's going to think you were in imminent danger? 10 feet? Was he stopped, or coming closer? Saying what, acting in what way? It isn't always so easy, especially after the fact, and when you weren't there to witness it yourself.

Someone running away from you is no longer a threat, even if they were a threat up until you pulled out a gun. Even if they just thoroughly beat the stuffing out of you! If it's over, it's over. You can't shoot someone for the purpose of punishment. That's what Law Enforcement and the courts are for. In most jurisdictions, Police Officers are allowed to use deadly force to prevent the escape of a violent felon, but citizens are not.

There are some jurisdictions that have a somewhat broader allowance for the use of deadly force – defense against carjacking and "stand your ground" and "castle" statutes come to mind, but if that's the case where you live, find out for sure, don't assume that because "you always heard" something that it's true.

Don't take seriously any ridiculous advice about "shoot him and drag him in the house" either. You may or may not be in the clear legally if you do get involved in a shooting, but touching anything having to do with the crime scene will not only be obvious to the investigators, but in court, any attempt you made to change or "sanitize" the crime scene will only guarantee your conviction.

Except - you ARE allowed to provide emergency first aid to someone you shoot, even encouraged to do so (if they are no longer a threat). You may end up saving the person's life, which will look a lot better in court than if you just stood there and watched the guy bleed to death, scumbag criminal or not. They or their family may still try to sue you. Criminally or civilly, you may be before a jury. You want the jury to know that YOU are a good person, with no bad intentions, did nothing wrong, and did everything right. Both juries if necessary.

Did I forget to mention that if you shoot at someone, as soon as the situation is safe for you to do so, you must call the police, and an ambulance would be a good idea if you actually hit someone. You really should report that you were involved in a shooting. Others may have heard the shot and called the police. If they have to find you the hard way, you will look very bad, indeed.

Someone can be standing outside your front door, banging and kicking and swearing up a storm. Call the police. As long as that door is between you and that lunatic, you're not in immediate danger. Shoot and you're going to jail. If you open that door thinking "now I can shoot this nut", guess what? As a juror, I'm going to think "this stupid guy opened his door to a maniac just so he could shoot him". Guilty as charged.

If your car is parked in front of your house, and you see a couple of thugs pounding it to scrap with sledgehammers, if you shoot them, you're going to jail. If you run out to try to stop them, and they then turn on you, in almost every jurisdiction I can think of, you aren't legally allowed to use deadly force. Why? You should have stayed in the house and waited for the police. Stopping these thugs is their business, not yours. It's only property. Malicious or not, there's no death penalty for property crimes. Your life wasn't in danger, only your property. You can't shoot people for destroying your ordinary property (note I say ordinary*). Deliberately putting yourself in a situation where you should have reasonably known your life could be put in danger, unfortunately, may erase your claim of self-defense.

(*Okay, as long as I mentioned it, depending on jurisdiction, all property is not alike. Your TV set is easily replaceable, your expensive and hard to replace work tools that you need in order to support your family is a bit different. A tank of oxygen is not just an ordinary tank of oxygen if it happens to be helping grandma breath and stay alive at the moment. There actually is a legal difference in the importance of property, but I'm not a lawyer, research it yourself. In all cases, the definition will really be based on the circumstances, and be up to the judge.)

A jury may find that any act that you take that inflames the situation, even merely getting involved in the first place, eliminates your right to use deadly force for self-defense. You can NEVER start a fight and then claim self-defense. Even if you are 100% in the right, you may still find yourself spending your life savings on lawyers to defend yourself, even if you avoid imprisonment.

Your best defense is to always do everything you reasonably can to avoid shooting. The police and the local prosecutor or District Attorney should be satisfied that it was a situation where you did not instigate the situation and had no reasonable choice but to shoot. They must be convinced, playing Monday morning quarterback, not having been there nor seen it themselves, that no one in your position would have had any choice. That still may not guarantee you'll avoid prosecution. Maybe the firearm or the bullets you used were too scary. Maybe you said the wrong thing to the police. Since joining the USCCA www.usconcealedcarry.com I've learned a few things, and I've put away my own scary looking Black Talon ammunition and carry only regular ball ammo now. Black Talon and "hollow points" in general have a reputation amongst the ignorant public that they are more "evil" than ball (plain, round) ammo, even though the potential for over penetration puts the rest of the public at more risk. Likewise, the decreased stopping power of ball ammo may also mean more shots may be required to stop an assailant, but it is what it is. Maybe hollow points are acceptable in Texas or Tennessee, but I live in Connecticut.

Face it, in our society, the anti-gun propagandists have tried their best to fill the general public with such lies and misinformation about guns that you may be prosecuted because the local District Attorney just doesn't like the idea of armed citizens running around on the loose no matter how justified you were.

You can use deadly force to save your own life, and you'll definitely know if you were in fear of your life, but if you use deadly force to save someone else's life, you'd better be damn sure that their life was really in danger!

The test is whether it is real – you'll have a heck of a time convincing a jury that you were saving someone's life if you happen to shoot someone who was "attacking" their friend with a rubber knife as a stupid prank. Even if you come upon a man smacking around a smaller woman on the street, you may learn what most police officers already know, in a domestic dispute like that, any outsider can be the enemy. Shoot the guy and the woman may not thank you for saving her, rather she may identify you in court as the maniac that killed her man for no good reason. What you perceived as a beating was just "fooling around", and they do it all the time.

Legally, nothing changes during an "event". The power has been out for a month, the stores have been closed just as long, and there's still no sign of the FEMA truck. Do you know if the current situation, assuming there is a breakdown in the social order, is permanent or temporary? If it's permanent, then by all means, feel free to join a mob, kill anyone who looks at you funny, and keep it up till some citizens finally kill you. If it's temporary, and you've unlawfully shot someone, then when things settle down and revert to some semblance of normalcy, expect a visit from law enforcement and a long vacation behind bars (or worse, depending on whether martial law is in effect). Whatever the situation, the rule still applies – you must be in fear that your life or the life of another is in immediate danger. To a moral and honorable person, taking a life will always be to save a life, no matter the circumstances. I'm not being a hypocrite, though. As I said, if I can't get more food, and you try to take my food from me, you are trying to kill me. I WILL use deadly force to protect my supply of food, and face the music later, if it ever comes.

I'm only going to discuss the situation inside your home. If you want to carry a firearm outside the home, you'll have to look into your local laws for yourself. If you decide that you want to assume the responsibility to protect yourself in your home, the first question is usually what kind of firearm do I get?

There are some Preppers who are ready for World War III, an alien invasion, or both. You might have seen them on TV. They're the ones who get to be on TV. Some experts will tell you to have a number of different firearms, for different purposes. If you're not already a gun owner, and know little about the subject, I recommend getting a shotgun. A basic, reliable pump action shotgun. Along with it, have someone at the gun store recommend where you can get some training with it. You probably don't belong to a rifle range, but the training will take place at one in your area anyway – you will be a guest of the trainer.

If you do not get safety training, and specific training in the use of the specific weapon you buy, you are apt to become the gun owner that the anti-gunners speak about when they discuss how dangerous it is to have a firearm at home, and how people tend to hurt or kill themselves or members of their family.

You need to actually use your shotgun, or whatever you end up buying. Know how to operate it, experience the results of firing it, and learn how to make it safe and clean it. Then you should find a way to occasionally practice with it. Some people say you should go to the range weekly, or at least a couple of times a month. I don't belong to a range, I tag along when I can with friends who have memberships, and I only get to practice several times a year. Then again, I'm not expecting to go into battle, I just want to maintain my familiarity and reinforce the good habits of gun handling. At some point, I may end up joining a range, and you may find you like shooting enough to do the same.

At some point, you might want to consider getting what would be considered a "battle" rifle, like an AR-15 variant, something that fires military-grade rifle rounds, with high capacity magazines of 10 to 30 rounds. If and when you make that decision, there's a wealth of information online to help you decide, or to completely confuse you. Look to YouTubers like Maineprepper to help guide you through the process.

If you do buy one, or any other firearm for that matter, also get a lockable trigger guard so the kids can't play with it. Many municipalities have a law requiring trigger locks on stored guns. Law or not, there are still big lawsuits and potential jail time for negligent homicide. Never leave an unsecured firearm of any type where kids can access it without you being there. There is NO hiding place that is safe for an unsecured firearm. Children may be small and ignorant, but they're not stupid, and you might think they don't know where you keep it, but I'd bet they do know. And guess what? They'll have a little friend, who has a friend, who will be able to get a hold of a bullet or shotgun shell (if they can't get one of yours). So keep it secure from the kids! When they're old enough to understand, get them some safety training, bring them to a range and teach (or have a professional teach) them safe gun handling, and eventually, even how to use the firearm (under close supervision). For that matter, get some professional training yourself!

Shotguns are not very complex, are slightly forgiving for mediocre accuracy (not very forgiving, at the distance involved for personal defense, the shot pattern will still be within the width of your hand), and there are a variety of shotgun shells for every model. A long gun does not usually have the same restrictions as a handgun, as it's not easily concealed, so it's going to be easier to get a long gun than a hand gun. Your local gun store will be able to guide you through the process.

A rifle, except for a ".22 caliber", will often be powerful enough that the bullet will travel through the wall of a room, through the outer wall of your home (unless it's brick, and even that might not stop it completely), then into the outer wall of your neighbor's home, and then possibly through your neighbor. Even if you hit your bad guy along the way, that bullet may still travel a lot farther than you want it to, and do something you wish it didn't do. A .22 may still penetrate a wall, but it will lose a lot of its momentum. The bad thing is that if you don't hit an assailant just right, it isn't powerful enough to stop an attacker. It's still a good rifle for target shooting, the ammunition is cheap, and it's good to practice with. It'll still kill if it hits the right part of the body, but the projectile doesn't have enough energy to knock down an assailant. You don't want to kill an assailant, you want to stop them from attacking you. You can pepper an assailant with .22 bullets and they may still have time to chop you into small pieces.

A shotgun, on the other hand, can be loaded with "shells" that contain the propellant (gunpowder) plus a variety of different types of projectiles, from a big fat plug (a "deer slug") to a few big balls ("buck shot") to a boatload of little tiny balls ("birdshot"). What I'm saying is that while you can't really ever call a shotgun shell "non-lethal", you can get shells that have more and lighter balls, that won't have the penetrating power of a rifle bullet but will still stop an assailant. Consult your gun store employee about your concerns, and if they're professional, they'll fix you up with exactly what you need for the situation you describe. They'll also be able to connect you with local training. It's worth it.

If they try to sell you a $2,000 fine hunting shotgun for home defense, go elsewhere. You shouldn't have to spend more than $250-500 for a basic home defense shotgun, and they might even be able to fix you up with a used one they took in on a trade for much less than that. A decent "battle" rifle, on the other hand, will start at $600-700, and go up from there. Expect to spend at least $1,000 or more with optional equipment.

I wouldn't bring a shotgun to the door any old time someone knocks, but if it's late, you're not expecting visitors, or if an event has occurred and the situation in your area is dangerous, answering the door (not opening, just answering) with a shotgun in hand will give a potential assailant pause for thought. That thinking might go like this: "Crap, he's/she's armed. I'll politely ask this guy if he has any food/gas/whatever to spare, then when he says no, I'll calmly walk away. There will always be another door to kick in and take everything they've got without risking my life".

That's if there is a window. If there's no window, they won't know you have a gun. Telling them you have a gun may or may not work, not to mention it'll sound pretty weird, unless they make threats to you. Perhaps the sound of you chambering a round in a pump shotgun will clue in any potential bad guy. In any case, at any time, in any circumstance, opening a door to a stranger is stupid. Hear out what they have to say and then tell them to get lost, or whatever else the situation calls for. If they need to call the police, or use your phone for any reason, make any calls for them. With the door closed. Better yet, call the police in any event, and let them help this person. Many people are dead because they opened their door to a stranger, and that's without being in an "event".

If it's an event and there's no phone, or no police, then by all means, let them know that you're armed. You can hear them out, but you probably can't help them anyway. If they go away, make sure they can't see in through any windows, and be on alert for the rest of the night, in case they didn't really go away. If you're in a situation where you have a group, and can be on the offensive, by all means send a couple of shooters sneaking out the back, so they can circle around and see what's going on. They must exit carefully just in case your visitors are covering the rear (or sides, whatever). If you don't have trained people, then just make sure that all the potential entrances to your home are covered. Someone may be keeping you busy in the front while accomplices are breaking into the rear.

Always remember that most residential doors and walls are no protection from high energy bullets. What you do about that is up to you and beyond the scope of this book, but the only thing a wall in your home will do is hide you from an assailant, not protect you. That works both ways.

If you're a couple, then each of you should have your own firearm. One of you can keep the other "covered". If you've got responsible teenagers at home, they can go through training with you. Having a couple of extra firearms in a gun safe "just in case" makes a lot of sense. If your home is attacked, the more people who can defend it the better. Predators want things to go easily their way. Just having a few gun barrels pointed in their direction might discourage them.

One armed person may discourage the casual dirtbag or two, but you can't cover the front, back, and both sides at the same time, day and night. If things really hit the fan, if it really gets to the point where there really are armed bands of marauders taking advantage of the lack of law enforcement, going around looting homes (whether occupied or not), you will not survive alone! You can't. You have to sleep. You'll have to go outdoors at some point. You will need, and hopefully there will be other armed citizens to band together with. Better to keep them out of your town than out of your house, or at least out of your neighborhood.

It would be great, if you can, to get involved in your town, volunteering for whatever opportunities are available in the spectrum from police and fire to emergency preparedness. You want to be part of the solution before there's really a problem, not to mention you want to be known as a positive, useful person in the community, not just some strange character hording food, just in case they decide someday that they need to get your stuff to redistribute. You would definitely want to be in on decision making like that from the get-go. As you learn more about preparedness, you can pass that knowledge on to the community leaders so they can begin thinking about what to do for the people in general. I've read many great articles on this subject, but the basic idea is that if you're collecting knowledge on how to survive, you can share that knowledge and be a part of someday helping the community survive as a group rather that a lot of individuals to be picked off one at a time – if it ever gets that bad.

I've joked about "feeding the unprepared neighbors or shooting them", but it's really no joke. Even though I'm not obligated to feed anyone else, I'd really much rather feed people than shoot them. At least as many as I comfortably can, for a period of time I comfortably can. Note I say "comfortably". I don't know if any of my neighbors are prepping. I may be the only one. Some neighbors, if I'm sharing my food with them, they will have other friends and neighbors who they'll tell, and they will have some, and so on. What if I'm the only one in the neighborhood with a stockpile of food? If I feed a half dozen folks one day, a couple of dozen may show up the next day. What if I wake up one morning to find a hundred people out there hoping for a meal?

If the FEMA trucks don't arrive in a reasonable amount of time, what am I to do? There will have to be a limit to the number of people I can feed, and those who come with their own arms and ammunition will necessarily top the list. Do you know what happens when unarmed people want what the armed people have? Be one of the armed people, not one of the sheeple. You can't eat guns, and you can't eat bullets. Food and guns go together. If you think that having a gun means you're going to take someone else's food, you may find that other people have bigger and better guns, and know how to use them more expertly. You should have both. If you can, you should convince the neighbors that it would be wise to have both, too.

Will things get back to normal, or not? If so, when? The first time you realize that calling the police, or attempting to call is futile, you'll know that it's time for citizens to defend themselves from lawlessness.

Some Preppers have an acronym called WROL, or "Without Rule of Law". That is a time period where there may be no organized law enforcement, if things have gotten really bad. If an event leads to WROL, the rules change, somewhat. You should still exhibit moral and honorable behavior, but the gloves come off when it comes to self-defense! The Monday morning quarterbacking will, if things get back to normal, only apply to the most extreme, egregious examples. There won't be a lot of micro evaluating going on, there will have been just too much death and destruction, especially in or near the cities.

Again, if you take my food, and I can't get more, I will starve. You will have killed me. If you try to kill me, I have the moral right to use deadly force to defend myself. If I honestly believe that I will not be able to get more food before I starve, that is the same as it being a fact, whether the FEMA trucks ever show up or not.

Don't worry, I won't be shooting my unarmed neighbors. Well, not if we're only in week 3 or 4, or even 5 of an event. I'm ensuring I can feed a lot of people for a short while by laying in 5 gallon pails of rice and beans (not forgetting the bouillon cubes for flavor). At the current prices of little more than a dollar a pound for properly packaged bulk dry goods, I can provide several hundred meals for much less than several hundred dollars. Feeding all and sundry for a limited time is good will. Doing the same till the food runs out is suicide.

Unfortunately, I won't have an unlimited amount of food. I'm not the federal government, able to borrow as much money as I want with no regard to paying it back. I can't afford to build the stockpile I'd ideally like to have. You would think the town would do that. If they are, they don't talk about it, but I doubt if they are so farsighted. If things don't look like they're going to get back to normal soon, the free ride will have to end. The sooner that happens, the fewer people who are eating out of my supplies, the longer the supplies will last. The reality is that cutting off armed people will result in a battle, one that I will likely lose. Cutting off the unarmed people may result in a battle, too, but distasteful as it sounds, it's a battle I doubt I'd lose, especially with a few other armed people on my side.

So guess who gets to survive, at least on my rations? The answer is the few armed people who will help me defend those supplies. At that point, the situation had better be permanent, because there's no going back once you have to turn people away to perhaps starve. Believe me, I've wrestled with these ideas for a couple of years, and I've come to the conclusion that I will be a survivor, if for no other reason than to see what things are like afterwards.

Your personal philosophy may that you must share out all of your supplies with everyone who shows up with their hand out, until there's nothing left to give. That's your business. You may think it's the right thing to do. Normally, it probably is, and you are, and always will be free to do so. You can "give till it hurts", even if that generosity means that you and your family end up starving to death long before there is a renewed food supply.

If you don't think you can live with yourself if you must turn away people to starve, then by all means, join them. If the situation is truly the end of life as we know it, or the "event" means no renewal of food supplies for many months, or more, the estimates I've read is that only 10-20% of the population will survive to do that farming I spoke about, anyway. You might not know it, or forgotten about it, or ignored it, but in the last century, due to famines in the Soviet Union, Communist China, and various other areas of the world, tens of millions of people have starved to death or died from the diseases that malnutrition invites. I'm not including war dead, just the dead from the criminal mismanagement of economies, sometimes because of unfortunate weather, or just the inability or lack of will to get food to people. Deaths because there wasn't enough food available at the time, just what we Preppers are trying to avoid. The situation continues to this very day in North Korea. Tens of millions, dead from starvation, well documented! Believe me, the death of you and your family will hardly be noted.

If it is my food, then I will decide who to share it with. I assure you that just being hungry with your hand out will be worth absolutely nothing to me. Come to me with an AR-15 and a couple of thousand rounds of ammunition, then that is worth something. Come with that and a hoard of survival food, and you are truly my brother. If we unite, we double our chances of survival. I don't know how many secret Preppers are in the neighborhood, but I won't be surprised to see many armed citizens coming out of the woodwork.

I live in a nation filled with people who have been trained that they will receive help whether they do anything to help themselves or not, it is somehow their inherent right to be helped. They are the "entitled" ones. The only problem they have is that they require a functioning government to do the dirty work of taking the hard earned wealth of others to provide them with that entitlement payment. If the event is such that there is no ability for the government to provide that essential service to them, they will have to do it themselves. That same lack of government means that there will be no protection for the "entitled" if the productive people decide to strenuously object to any more redistribution efforts that aren't from the goodness of their hearts. I know that my objection will be very strenuous, indeed.

I leave now you to ponder your future.

Shopping Links

Here are a bunch of food and equipment shopping links for your convenience. Some of these I already mentioned, others are only in their applicable chapter. I take no responsibility for these links and do not explicitly recommend any except Emergency Essentials, with whom I've been doing business for a couple of years, with consistently happy results. Many of these sites provide very useful articles for self-education as well. I didn't bother including companies that only provide expensive package deals, with little or no provision for sampling the items. They advertise heavily, and expect you to jump right in for hundreds or thousands of dollars. Want to invest $100 for 93 servings of apple juice mix? Didn't think so.

www.beprepared.com

 www.nitro-pak.com

   http://www.augasonfarms.com

www.Survivalacres.com

www.alpineair.com

www.honeyvillegrain.com (originator of bulk basic ingredients, not ready made meals)

www.thereadystore.com

www.usaemergencysupply.com

www.stpaulmercantile.com This is where I got my kerosene stove.

www.readymaderesources.com Can't copy their logo.

Perhaps one of the most useful preparedness guides is a compilation by Christopher M. Parrett. It's made up of articles and posts from discussion groups that he collected over time, and distributes it as both a printed version where you just pay for the cost of production and postage, or a pdf version that is freely available at www.ldsavow.com There's about 500 pages of useful stuff covering a very wide range of topics, including some I only alluded to here.

Made in the USA
San Bernardino, CA
25 April 2014